Book 6
Teacher's Guide and Answer Key

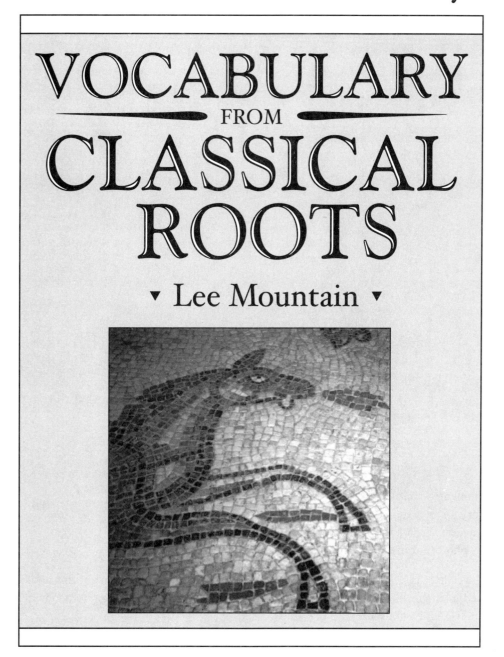

EDUCATORS PUBLISHING SERVICE
Cambridge and Toronto

Acquisitions/Development: Sethany Rancier Alongi
Editor: Mary Troeger
Senior Editorial Manager: Sheila Neylon
Typesetter and cover photo: Sarah Cole

© 2006 by School Specialty, Inc. All rights reserved. Except as authorized below, no part of this book may be reproduced or utilized in any form or by any electronic or mechanical means, including photocopying, without permission in writing from the publisher.

The purchase of this book entitles the buyer to reproduce designated pages for instructional use. Reproduction for an entire school system or for commercial use is prohibited without written permission.

Printed in Benton Harbor, MI, in March 2017
ISBN 978-0-8388-2251-7

9 10 11 12 13 PPG 21 20 19 18 17

CONTENTS

Introduction iv

Lesson Plan Format iv

Selection Criteria: Why These Words and Roots? v

Additional Word-Learning Strategies vi

Lesson 1: Seeing 1

Lesson 2: Hearing 5

Lesson 3: Speaking 9

Lesson 4: Reviewing Lessons 1–3 13

Lesson 5: Writing 17

Lesson 6: Connecting 21

Lesson 7: Lowering (with Prefixes) 24

Lesson 8: Reviewing Lessons 5–7 28

Lesson 9: Sending 33

Lesson 10: Turning 36

Lesson 11: Handling 40

Lesson 12: Reviewing Lessons 9–11 43

Lesson 13: Belonging 47

Lesson 14: Illuminating 51

Lesson 15: Changing (with Suffixes) 55

Lesson 16: Reviewing Lessons 13–15 59

Reproducible Worksheets: Word Activity Masters 63

Answers to Word Activity Masters 75

Word List 80

INTRODUCTION

This teacher's guide for *Vocabulary from Classical Roots 6* complements, extends, and enriches the lessons of the student book in three ways.

First, the lesson plans help students to access prior knowledge, thereby enabling them to make connections between familiar words and new words that share the same classical root. For example, the familiar word *scribble*, with its root *scrib*, can provide scaffolding for learning the related words *scribe* and *prescribe*.

Second, the lesson plans provide a variety of *oral* activities as well as additional written activities on reproducible worksheets. Discussions and games (classroom contests, synonym tic-tac-toe, charades, word puzzles, syllable sorts) lead students to incorporate the new words into their oral and written vocabularies.

Third, the lesson plans expand students' understanding of *classical roots*, the unique focus of this series. They provide teachers with a sensible and effective way to teach vocabulary from a roots-based perspective, even when a background in classical-language roots is not a part of the teacher's own experience. The knowledge of Latin and Greek roots can give students a head start on unlocking the meanings of innumerable words they will meet in the intermediate and secondary grades.

LESSON PLAN FORMAT

The lesson plans in this guide for all lessons (except review lessons) have the following headings.

Introduce Lesson

Before your students pick up their pencils, *talk* with them about the lesson title and the two featured roots or affixes.

Preview Familiar Words

Through *oral* activities, show students how the featured roots relate to the meanings of the familiar words.

Present Key Words

Build *oral* familiarity with the key words. Then have students read the words, underline the featured roots, use root clues to help with meanings, and study the full definitions.

Guide Oral Practice

Give students opportunities to use the words *orally* in two activities: "Connections and Examples" and "Draw, Display, Discuss."

Assign Written Exercises

Have students match synonyms and antonyms, fill in key words in context, and work with related roots and affixes.

Answer keys are provided for all exercises.

A reproducible worksheet for additional reinforcement is also provided for each lesson (except the review lessons). These worksheets are located at the end of this guide (see pages 63–74).

The lesson plans for all of the review lessons in this guide have these headings:

Discuss

Use oral activities for revisiting the vocabulary from the preceding three lessons.

Reinforce

Use oral activities for further practice with the material presented in each Exercise C.

Explore

Use additional word-learning strategies to review specific words (see pages vi–viii).

Guide Oral Practice

Organize classroom games such as Definition Challenge and Charades.

Assign Written Exercises

Reinforce vocabulary with activities that expand associations with words, roots, and affixes.

Answer keys are provided for the exercises.

SELECTION CRITERIA: WHY THESE WORDS AND ROOTS?

For any vocabulary textbook, the initial questions are: *which* words and *why* these words?

For answers, look at the title of this book, *Vocabulary from **Classical Roots** 6*. All the featured words are derived from classical roots. Knowing even a limited number of Latin and Greek roots can provide clues to the meanings of an unlimited number of multisyllabic words.

So, the questions for this book have to be: *which* roots and *why* these roots? For answers, look at the three selection criteria for deciding which classical roots to include: frequency, usefulness, and research.

Frequency

Roots that appear on lists of the 3000 most frequently used words were chosen, along with some prefixes and suffixes derived from Latin and Greek. These parts of words recur often in vocabulary across the curriculum.

Usefulness

From the secondary books of the *Vocabulary from Classical Roots* series, it was easy to ascertain which roots, prefixes, and suffixes were expected to be known from the intermediate grades. These meaningful parts are featured in the books for grades 5 and 6, along with some roots that were presented at an advanced level, but are useful to intermediate students when given a simpler presentation.

Research

Publications by vocabulary authorities provided research findings as well as expert opinions on the roots and affixes that could best help intermediate students figure out word meanings. Also the research underlying student dictionaries was helpful in determining which roots, prefixes, suffixes, and definitions were most suitable for the intermediate grades.

Now that you know the *why* behind the selection of words and roots in this book, let's return to the initial questions:

Which words? See the list on the last page.

Which roots? See the inside front cover.

ADDITIONAL WORD-LEARNING STRATEGIES

The following word-learning strategies can be adapted for individual, small group, or whole class instruction. They are helpful in focusing attention on a particular prefix, root, or word. As students expand their word webs, fill in their Venn diagrams, and answer questions for their definition maps, they are deepening their understanding of the new words in their vocabularies.

WEBS WITH ROOTS AND AFFIXES

A root or affix web can help students identify the meaning common to a group of words. Display the root or affix in the middle of the web and discuss its meaning. Complete the web with words that contain the root or affix. Students can include different forms of the same word. Discuss definitions and relationships of the words to the root or affix.

The graphic can be as simple as the following web with *audi,* showing just a few words connected to the root, or as complex as the web with *gen,* featuring groups of related words.

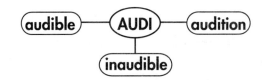

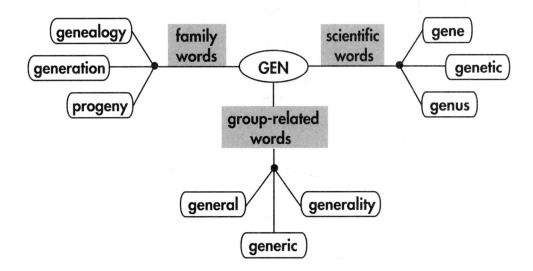

VENN DIAGRAMS

The overlapping circles of a Venn diagram can show how two words are similar and different. In the first Venn diagram below, the differences between *saxophone* and *megaphone* are listed in the outer parts of the circles. The similarities are listed in the overlapping section in the middle. In the second Venn diagram, the same procedure is followed for the words *autograph* and *biography*.

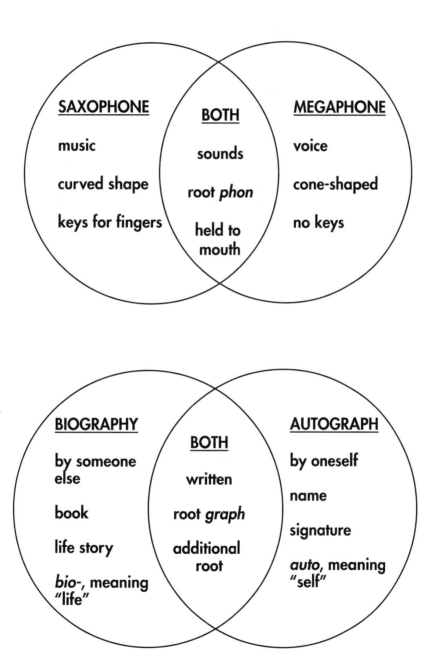

DEFINITION MAP

A definition map is a visual display that shows the common components of a dictionary definition by answering these questions about a word:

What is it?

What is it like?

What are some specific examples of the word?

What are some specific non-examples of the word?

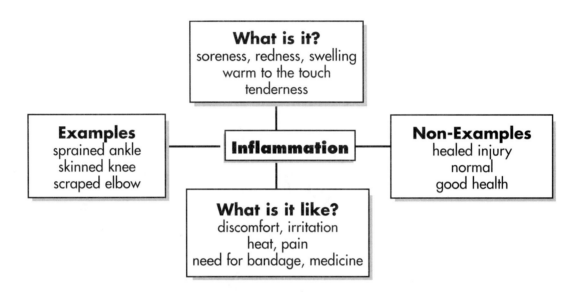

Independently or in groups, students can fill in the map and then use the information to write an expanded definition of the word, based on the map. For example: Inflammation is an uncomfortable condition that can be brought on by an injury, such as a sprained ankle or a skinned knee. The area of inflammation often looks red, feels warm, and shows swelling.

LESSON 1: SEEING

LESSON 1: SEEING (PAGES 1–5)

> ### Key Words
>
> envision   prospect   respect   revise
> spectacle   spectacular spectator supervise
> visible   visor

INTRODUCE LESSON 1

(page 1) Introduce Lesson 1 orally by having students read the title "Seeing" and the two featured roots *vis*, meaning "see," and *spect*, meaning "look at." Clearly, the meanings overlap.

Ask students how they protect or improve their vision. (Examples: glasses, contacts, sunglasses, laser corrections of nearsightedness, proper nutrition)

Have they heard the word *spectacles*? What does it mean? (It is an old-fashioned name for eyeglasses.)

PREVIEW FAMILIAR WORDS

(pages 1, 2) *vision, visit, visual, inspect, suspect*

Activity 1: *vis*

Display the familiar words *vision, visit,* and *visual*. Read them orally and then chorally with the class. Underline the root *vis* in each one.

Ask students the following questions:

Which familiar word is a synonym of *sight*? (*vision*)

Which familiar word refers to "going to *see*" someone? (*visit*)

If I say that a design has *visual* appeal, what do I mean? (You mean that you like what you *see*; the design is pleasing to the eyes.)

Ask: What is the shared meaning for the root *vis* in the words *visit, vision,* and *visual*? (seeing, sight)

Activity 2: *spect*

Display the familiar words *inspect* and *suspect*. Read the words orally and then chorally with the class. Underline the root *spect* in each word.

Ask students the following questions:

What do you do when you inspect an item? (You *look at* it carefully.)

VOCABULARY FROM CLASSICAL ROOTS

Suppose you come home from school to find many things in one room all messed up and out of order. You wonder who or what did this. If you also have a pet dog or some younger brothers and sisters, you may have an idea of who or what caused the mess. What do we call the person or animal that we are *looking at* as the possible cause of the mess before we know for certain? (suspect)

Ask: What is the shared meaning for the root *spect* in *inspect* and *suspect*? (look at)

PRESENT KEY WORDS

Display the key words. Read them orally and chorally with the class.

Have students underline the root in each key word in the box on page 1; then have them check to be sure that their words look like this.

en<u>vis</u>ion	pro<u>spect</u>	re<u>spect</u>	re<u>vise</u>
<u>spect</u>acle	<u>spect</u>acular	<u>spect</u>ator	super<u>vise</u>
<u>vis</u>ible	<u>vis</u>or		

Ask students the following questions:

Which words begin with a root? (*spectacle, spectacular, spectator, visible, visor*)

Which words have a prefix before the root? (*envision, prospect, respect, revise, supervise*)

In Exercise C, you will find out more about the prefix *super-*. For now, just try to predict the meaning of *super-*. (probably "big, above, over," and other similar meanings) Why do you predict those meanings? (Answers will vary. Examples: Superman was *big* and strong. A super bowler is one whose score is *above*, or higher than, the scores of the other bowlers. Superheroes can jump *over* tall buildings.)

As students complete the "Using Root Clues" section, encourage them to use the meanings of the roots to find the correct answer. Have them match the columns <u>before</u> they study the complete definitions of the words.

Dictate the answers so that students can check themselves.

(page 1) 1. D   2. B   3. A   4. C

Present each key word, paying attention to pronunciation, part of speech, definition with context sentence, and other parts of the listing as applicable (additional derivation, related word form, illustration).

In this first lesson, take time to introduce students to the respellings that help with pronunciation.

Ask: On page 1, what letters and symbols do you see in the parentheses following the word *envision*? (the letters i n v i z h n and the symbol schwa, which looks like an upside down *e*) What is the sound of the schwa? (uh as in *about*) What is the purpose of respelling *envision*? (to show how the word is pronounced)

How many syllables do you hear in envision? (three) Which syllable is accented, or said

LESSON 1: SEEING

most loudly? (the second syllable, *vi*) In the respelling, where do you see the accent mark? (after the second syllable, to show that it is the accented syllable)

Many respellings use marks other than the accent mark. Look back at the inside front cover to see the "Key to Diacritical Marks." These marks help with pronunciation.

Which four vowels have long marks, or lines called macrons, over them? (*a, e, i,* and *o*)

Look at the first letter of the key word that follows each vowel—*apron, even, ivy,* and *open.* In each case, what do you notice about the sound of the initial letter? (It is the same as the name of the letter.) What is the respelling of the long sound of *u*? (The letter *y* followed by the two-dot *u*)

What other vowel is shown with two dots over it? (*a*) What is the sound of the two-dot *a*? (ah, as in *father*)

Look again at the respelling of *envision* on page 1. If you had no previous acquaintance with this word, would the respelling enable you to pronounce it correctly? (yes)

At the top of page 2, what does the respelling of *revise* tell you about the sounds of the first two vowels in the word? (They are both long, so they sound like the names of the letters.)

GUIDE ORAL PRACTICE
Activity 1: Connections and Examples

Ask students for some examples of *spectacular* sights they have experienced. (Answers will vary but will probably include natural wonders, artistic creations, performances of different kinds.) Why were these *spectacles* so impressive? (Answers will vary but will probably emphasize size, color, organization, and so on.)

Explain that sometimes there is a strong connection between the meaning of a word and the meaning of its root. The connection is very easy to see. Other times the connection is not quite as close, so it does not come to mind as quickly.

The root *vis* makes people think of vision, and therefore of seeing. Which word has a closer connection with the idea of seeing: *visible* or *revise*? (*Visible,* since it means "able to be seen." To *revise* is to look at again and change, and "looking at" is certainly related to "seeing," but usually the first connection that jumps to mind for revising is *changing,* rather than *seeing.*)

What part of speech is the word *vision*? (noun) When you add the prefix *en-* to *vision,* it is no longer a noun. What part of speech is the word *envision,* as in "I envision happy futures for all of you"? (verb) What achievements do you envision for yourselves in high school? (Examples: good grades, athletic success, leading a project)

At what event have you recently been a *spectator*? (Answers may range from athletic events to live performances.) You usually think of the members of a football, basketball, soccer, or baseball team as players or participants, not spectators. When, during each game, are some team members acting as spectators? (when they are on the bench or in the dugout, watching the other players in action)

VOCABULARY FROM CLASSICAL ROOTS

Activity 2: Draw, Display, Discuss

Display a cap or headband with a *visor*. Have students show or describe visors they wear. Where is a visor that you do <u>not</u> wear on your head? (There is one in the car above the windshield. You pull down that visor to shield your eyes from the glare.)

Ask: Have any of you ever *supervised* younger children? (Probably some students can tell about their supervising of younger siblings. Maybe a few can report on babysitting.)

When you supervised, *what* did you direct or oversee? (probably the behavior of the younger child in terms of eating, television-viewing, adhering to bedtime)

List some people you *respect*. What is it about each of them that you respect and admire? (Answers will vary.)

What are some *prospects* you have for the next school vacation? (Answers will vary but may include a vacation trip with the family, doing things with friends, and so on.)

ASSIGN WRITTEN EXERCISES
Exercise A: Synonyms (pages 3–4)

1. b 2. c 3. a 4. d 5. a

Exercise B: Meaning in Context (page 4)

1. supervised 2. respect 3. prospect 4. visible 5. spectacular

Exercise C: Extend Your Vocabulary (pages 4–5)

1. C 2. E 3. A 4. B 5. D
6. B 7. A 8. E 9. C 10. D

Reproducible Worksheet: Lesson 1 (page 63 in this book)

LESSON 2: HEARING

LESSON 2: HEARING (PAGES 6–10)

> ### Key Words
>
> | | | | |
> |---|---|---|---|
> | audible | audience | audition | auditorium |
> | inaudible | megaphone | phonics | saxophone |
> | stereophonic | symphony | | |

INTRODUCE LESSON 2

(page 6) Introduce Lesson 2 orally by having students read the title "Hearing" and the two featured roots *audi,* meaning "listening, hearing," and *phon,* meaning "sounds." To show students the close connection of the two featured roots, point out that "ear*phones*" are classified as "*audio* aids." The sciences of sounds and hearing are called *phon*ology and *audi*ology.

Ask: What roots do you hear in the words *phonology* and *audiology*? (*phon* and *audi*)

PREVIEW FAMILIAR WORDS

(pages 6, 7) *audiobook, audiotape, audiovisual, microphone, phone, telephone*

Activity 1: *audi*

Display the familiar words *audiobook, audiotape,* and *audiovisual.* Read them orally and then chorally with the class. Underline the root *audi* in each one.

Ask students the following questions:

What is the difference between an audiobook and a bound book? (A bound book is printed on paper for you to read. An audiobook is a recording on audiotape of someone reading a book aloud so that people can *listen* to it.)

Is the overhead projector, which is used in many classrooms, an audiovisual aid? (no) Why not? (We can look at what it projects, but we do not *hear* any sounds from it. It is a visual aid, but not an *audio*visual aid.)

Is an audiotape an audiovisual aid? (It is an audio aid, since we can hear it when it is played on the tape recorder, but it is not audio*visual*; it does not produce anything for people to see.)

You met the root *vis* in Lesson 1. What does it mean? (see) Which of our senses does an audiovisual aid reach? (the sense of sight and the sense of hearing) Name some audiovisual aids. (films, computer programs, DVDs)

Ask: What are the shared meanings for the root *audi* in the words *audiobook, audiotape,* and *audiovisual*? (listening, hearing)

VOCABULARY FROM CLASSICAL ROOTS

Activity 2: *phon*

Display the familiar words *microphone, phone,* and *telephone.* Read them orally and then chorally with the class. Underline the root *phon* in each one.

Ask students the following questions:

What is the purpose of a microphone? (to make *sounds* louder, and therefore easier to hear)

What do you hear on the telephone (often shortened to the word *phone*)? (the *sound* of the voice of the person talking to you)

Ask: What is the shared meaning for the root *phon* in the words *microphone, phone,* and *telephone?* (sound)

PRESENT KEY WORDS

Display the key words. Read them orally and then chorally with the class.

Have students underline the root in each key word in the box on page 6; then have them check to be sure that their words look like this.

audible	audience	audition	auditorium
inaudible	megaphone	phonics	saxophone
stereophonic	symphony		

Ask students the following questions:

Which key words begin with a root? (*audible, audience, audition, auditorium, phonics*)

Which key word begins with a prefix that means "not"? (*inaudible*) Since *audible* means "able to be heard," what do you think *inaudible* means? (not able to be heard) What do you call the words *audible* and *inaudible*? (antonyms, because they are opposites.)

Which four key words that contain the root *phon* do not begin with that root? (*megaphone, saxophone, stereophonic, symphony*) Which two of these words are types of horns? (*megaphone* and *saxophone*)

As students complete the "Using Root Clues" section, encourage them to use the meanings of the roots to find the correct answer. Have them match the columns before they study the complete definitions of the words.

Dictate the answers so that students can check themselves.

(page 6) 1. D   2. C   3. A   4. B

Present each key word, paying attention to pronunciation, part of speech, definition with context sentence, and other parts of the listing as applicable (additional derivation, related word form, illustration).

Point out that the word *audition* (page 7) can be used as a noun or a verb, so definitions and sentences are provided for both parts of speech. Have students compose a sentence in which *audition* appears as a verb and as a noun. (Example: He wanted to *audition* for

LESSON 2: HEARING

the role of the hero, so he rehearsed the speech he would use in his *audition*.)

Have students look at the word *symphony* (page 8), which has an additional derivation, given in the brackets that follow the pronunciation. The word has two meaningful parts: the Greek *sym* as well as the featured root *phon*. What is the meaning of *sym*? (together) What is the meaning of *phon*? (sounds) Literally, what meaning do those two parts convey? (sounds together) At the end of the listing for *symphony* is its related adjective form, *symphonic*. Can you think of any other adjectives that end in *-ic*? (Examples: *angelic, photographic, microscopic*) At a performance of a symphonic work, how many musicians would you expect to participate? (a large number, as in an orchestra)

GUIDE ORAL PRACTICE

Activity 1: Connections and Examples

Have students name various instruments in the orchestra that might play parts of a *symphony*. (Accept all answers that name traditional instruments. Point out that some instruments not generally included in an orchestra, like the harmonica or banjo, may be included for a specific symphony.)

Which key word do you connect with learning to read in the primary grades? (*phonics*)

What did you study in phonics? (the sounds of letters of the alphabet) Do some letters stand for more than one sound? (Yes, each vowel has at least a long and a short sound, and the schwa sound can be spelled with many different letters.)

Most of you give your oral reports in good strong voices that are *audible* to the whole room. But some students occasionally speak in soft voices that are *inaudible*; then you can't hear the speaker. What should you do if a speaker's voice is inaudible? (Raise your hand, and say, "Please speak louder.")

What was your favorite program so far this year in our school *auditorium*? Why did you especially enjoy being in the *audience*? Where else, besides school, have you been in an auditorium? (perhaps at a civic center, a theater, or a hotel)

Why are *auditions* often held in auditoriums? (to test whether the performers, who are trying out for roles, can make themselves heard throughout a large space)

Activity 2: Draw, Display, Discuss

Which of the key words is easiest to make as a model? (probably *megaphone*, since you can make one by rolling paper into a cone-shaped voice amplifier) Where might you see larger, heavier megaphones? (in the hands of cheerleaders at games)

Where have you heard *stereophonic* sound? (maybe at home through two or more speakers, in movie theaters)

To be chosen for a part in a play, you need to *audition*, or try out, for the part. Have any of you auditioned? Tell about the experience.

Where might you see or hear a *saxophone*? (Answers will vary; some students may actually own and play a saxophone.)

VOCABULARY FROM CLASSICAL ROOTS

Nota Bene: The word *saxophone* can be called an "eponym," since it derived its name from the Belgian inventor A. J. Sax (1814–94), just as the sousaphone was named for John Philip Sousa (1854–1932), the American bandleader and composer of marches.

ASSIGN WRITTEN EXERCISES

Exercise A: Synonyms (page 8)

1. b   2. d   3. c   4. a   5. c

Exercise B: Meaning in Context (page 9)

1. auditions   2. auditorium   3. audible   4. inaudible   5. audience

Exercise C: Extend Your Vocabulary (pages 9–10)

1. aquarium   2. terrarium   3. emporium   4. planetarium   5. solarium
6. planet   7. terr   8. solar   9. aqua   10. place

Reproducible Worksheet: Lesson 2 (page 64 in this book)

LESSON 3: SPEAKING (PAGES 11–15)

> ### Key Words
>
> addictive   avocation   contradict   dictation
> dictator   predict   verdict   vocal
> vocalist   vocation

INTRODUCE LESSON 3

(page 11) Introduce Lesson 3 orally by having students read the title "Speaking," and the two featured roots *voc*, meaning "words, voice, calling," and *dict*, meaning "to speak or say." Point out that these roots often overlap and share meanings. Consider the words *voc*abulary and *dict*ionary. Both are connected with words, so the roots *voc* and *dict* are related.

PREVIEW FAMILIAR WORDS

(pages 11, 12) *vocabulary, dictate, dictionary*

Activity 1: *voc*

Display the familiar word *vocabulary*. Read it orally and then chorally with the class. Underline the root *voc*.

Ask students the following questions:

You have many vocabularies: your listening vocabulary, your speaking vocabulary, your writing vocabulary, your reading vocabulary. Which one do you think you developed first? (The listening vocabulary is first. Toddlers can listen and follow *spoken* directions even before they start talking.) Which vocabularies did you develop second, third, and fourth? (The speaking vocabulary comes second, the reading vocabulary comes third, and the writing fourth.)

Which do you think is bigger—your writing or reading vocabulary? (Usually, at this point in school, students' reading vocabularies will be larger. They understand *words* that they meet while reading long before they start using all those *words* in their writing.)

Ask: What is the meaning of the root *voc* in the word *vocabulary*? (words)

Activity 2: *dict*
Display the familiar words *dictate* and *dictionary*. Read them orally and then chorally with the class. Underline *dict* in each one.

Ask students the following questions:

What is a dictionary? (a book that gives information about words)

What connection does a dictionary have with speaking or saying? (In addition to giving the meanings of words, dictionary listings tell you how to *say* the word correctly.) Where does that part appear? (in parentheses, right after the word) Why is the word respelled and marked with diacritical marks? (Many letters of the English alphabet stand for more than one sound, so you need the respelling and marking to show you the correct way to *say* the word.)

What do you do when you dictate? (You either *speak* aloud so that someone can write down what you say, or you give orders, *say*ing what others must do.)

Ask: What is the shared meaning for the root *dict* in the words *dictionary* and *dictate*? (speak or say)

PRESENT KEY WORDS

Display the key words. Read them orally and then chorally with the class.

Have students underline the root in each key word in the box on page 11; then have them check to be sure that their words look like this.

ad<u>dict</u>ive	a<u>voc</u>ation	contra<u>dict</u>	<u>dict</u>ation
<u>dict</u>ator	pre<u>dict</u>	ver<u>dict</u>	<u>voc</u>al
<u>voc</u>alist	<u>voc</u>ation		

Ask students the following questions:

Which key words start with a root? (*dictation, dictator, vocal, vocalist, vocation*)

Which ones end with the root *dict*? (*contradict, predict, verdict*)

Look at the word *addictive*. You know that *dict* is the root. What do you call the meaningful part *ad-* that you see at the beginning of the word? (a prefix) What do you call the *-ive* that you see at the end of the word? (a suffix) How many meaningful parts do you see in *addictive*? (three, a prefix, a root, and a suffix)

The prefix *ad-* means "to" or "toward"; the root *dict* means "say"; the suffix *-ive* signals that the word is an adjective. If you cover the suffix *-ive*, what word is left? (*addict*) What is an addict? (a person who says *yes* to habit-forming substances)

You may find that you are familiar with a related form of another of the key words. You probably know that a weather *prediction* is "telling what tomorrow's weather will be like before tomorrow arrives." So, can you figure out what *predict* means? (to tell before)

As students complete the "Using Root Clues" section, encourage them to use the meanings of the roots to find the correct answers. Have them match the columns <u>before</u> they study the complete definitions of the words.

Dictate the answers so that students can check themselves.

LESSON 3: SPEAKING

(page 11) 1. D   2. A   3. B   4. C

Present each key word, paying attention to pronunciation, part of speech, definition with context sentence, and other parts of the listing as applicable (additional derivation, related word form, illustration).

Point out to students that knowing a key word will help them understand its related forms. On pages 12 and 13, these related forms of key words appear after the example sentences.

At the end of the entry for *vocal* is the related adverb, *vocally*.

At the end of the entry for *addictive* are the related nouns *addiction* and *addict*.

At the end of the entry for *contradict* is the related noun, *contradiction*.

At the end of the entry for *predict* are the related noun *prediction* and the related adjective *predictable*.

Have students practice using the related forms in sentences that show the connection to the meaning of the root.

The *Nota Bene* for *vocation* and *avocation* mentions that these words can overlap in meaning when people truly love their work. Robert Frost's poem, "Two Tramps in Mud Time," examines the tension between vocation and avocation. He writes, "But yield who will to their separation,/ My object in living is to unite/ My avocation and my vocation/ As my two eyes make one in sight."

GUIDE ORAL PRACTICE
Activity 1: Connections and Examples

A *vocation* is "a calling" to a particular type of work. What jobs take so many years of schooling that a person would have to feel *called* to them, to put in all the training time? (Doctor probably will be among the first answers, along with astronaut, various scientists, lawyer, professor, and so on.)

Which key word contains the word *vocation*? (*avocation*) Some people call an avocation "a hobby that you work at." Avocations are hobbies or activities that interest people intensely. Give examples of some avocations. (Answers will vary but probably will include various sports, creative activities, and games.)

Teachers sometimes dictate sentences for students to write in their notebooks. Have you ever taken *dictation* in class? If so, what did you write? (Often, the dictation will be just a short note to take home to parents, as a reminder of a meeting perhaps.)

When I say the word *dictator*, what is your first thought? (probably, a person who takes complete control of a country, or a situation, often without consent, in order to tell others what to do) Why is it often dangerous to *contradict* a dictator? (because such a person has complete power in the country and will usually use it against any who provide opposition)

VOCABULARY FROM CLASSICAL ROOTS

Activity 2: Draw, Display, Discuss

Ask students to bring in pictures of popular vocalists for display. Have them demonstrate how a vocalist might deliver a song. Do their favorite *vocalists* usually sing alone or with musical backup? (Answers will vary. Have them identify the most common instruments used for backup for their vocalists.)

A *verdict* is the decision of a jury, but it can also be used for decisions made by other groups. What are some television programs where audiences give a verdict? (Answers will vary.)

ASSIGN WRITTEN EXERCISES

Exercise A: Synonyms (pages 13–14)

1. d   2. c   3. a   4. b   5. d

Exercise B: Meaning in Context (page 14)

1. addictive   2. contradict   3. vocation   4. avocation   5. vocalist

Exercise C: Extend Your Vocabulary (pages 14–15)

1. prefix   2. preview   3. prehistoric   4. precedes   5. prevent

Reproducible Worksheet: Lesson 3 (page 65 in this book)

LESSON 4: REVIEWING LESSONS 1–3 (PAGES 16–20)

Before your students do the written review exercises in the book, conduct an oral review of the meanings of the featured roots and prefixes, the word parts introduced in each Exercise C, and the key vocabulary from Lessons 1, 2, and 3.

DISCUSS

Use these kinds of questions to challenge students.

In what words do the meanings of *voc* and *dict* overlap? (Examples: In *vocabulary* and *dictionary*, the roots *voc* and *dict* both mean "words." In the sentence, "The dictator is very vocal about what he expects done," both roots are related to speaking.) Lesson 3

Give some words that connect the "sounds" meaning of *phon* with musical sounds. (Examples: *symphony, saxophone, microphone, symphonic, stereophonic*) Lesson 2

What is the connection in meaning between the words *spectator* and *spectacle*? (They both have the *spect* root, which can mean "look at, sight." A *spectator* can be surprised to look upon an amazing sight, a *spectacle*.) Lesson 1

When is a *vocation* also an *avocation*? (when you love your work so much that you do it for pleasure as well as for a salary) Lesson 3

Think of a three-syllable word that means "try out" or "have a hearing, for a part." (*audition*) What part of that word gives you the "hearing" clue? (the root *audi*) Lesson 2

REINFORCE

The word *predict* starts with the prefix *pre-*. What does this prefix mean? (before) Use *predict* in a sentence that shows the "before" connection. (Example: Before each baseball game, I predict that our home team will win, but my predictions do not always turn out to be correct.) Lesson 3

What meaning do you associate with the suffix *-orium/-arium*? (place) Name some places that end in that suffix. (auditorium, aquarium, planetarium, terrarium, solarium, emporium, sanatorium) Lesson 2

Explain how one of these *-orium/-arium* places is related in meaning to its root. (An aquarium is a place filled with *water*, and the root *aqua* means "water.") Lesson 2

What word that starts with *super-* is the antonym of *inferior*? (superior) Lesson 1

Which word with the prefix *super-* is the name for a road with many lanes for cars? (a superhighway) Use that word in a sentence. (Example: The superhighway near our school is always full of traffic.) Lesson 1

EXPLORE

When students would benefit from a more in-depth exploration of a particular word, the additional word-learning strategies at the beginning of this book (pages vi–viii) can be helpful.

VOCABULARY FROM CLASSICAL ROOTS

GUIDE ORAL PRACTICE

Activity 1: Definition Challenge

Give each student a card (3" by 5" or 5" by 7"). Assign each student one of the thirty words from the box at the top of page 17 in the student book. Have the student copy the complete definition of that word on the card. Line up the class in two teams, facing each other.

The first student on Team A reads a definition. The first student on Team B can earn two points by coming up with the word that fits the definition. If the answer is incorrect, Team B may still earn one point if another member can come up with the word.

The teams take turns until all the definitions have been read. The team with the most points wins.

Activity 2: Charades (sorting by parts of speech)

Hand each student another blank card (3" by 5" or 5" by 7"). Again assign to each student one of the thirty words, but make sure it is a different one from the word the student had for Activity 1. The student will copy the new word and its full definition from the book.

Write these categories on the board: nouns, verbs, adjectives, nouns and verbs. Tell students to sort themselves into these four groups, according to the part of speech of their assigned words, and to line up in alphabetical order. Their groupings should look like this:

Nouns	**Verbs**	**Adjectives**	**Nouns and Verbs**
audience	contradict	addictive	audition
auditorium	envision	audible	prospect
avocation	predict	inaudible	respect
dictation	revise	spectacular	
dictator	supervise	stereophonic	
megaphone		visible	
phonics		vocal	
saxophone			
spectacle			
spectator			
symphony			
verdict			
visor			
vocalist			
vocation			

LESSON 4: REVIEWING LESSONS 1–3

Let the students holding the words *audition, prospect,* and *respect* join the verb group. Divide the group of nouns in half so that the groups will be fairly evenly divided.

Tell each group to select two of their words to act out, as in charades. Allow a little time for each group to plan what they will do. All of the group's words should stay on display while the acting is taking place. The other students have to guess which word is being portrayed.

Activity 3: Charades (sorting by syllables)

Have each student give his or her word card from the previous activity to another student.

Tell students to sort themselves into new groups, according to the number of syllables in their word. Then, have each group line up in alphabetical order, while holding up their cards. Their groupings should look like this:

Two	Three	Four	Five
phonics	addictive	avocation	auditorium
predict	audible	inaudible	stereophonic
prospect	audience	spectacular	
respect	audition		
revise	contradict		
verdict	dictation		
visor	dictator		
vocal	envision		
	megaphone		
	saxophone		
	spectacle		
	spectator		
	supervise		
	symphony		
	visible		
	vocalist		
	vocation		

Combine the groups with words of four and five syllables. Break the three-syllable group in half. Proceed as above, with each group planning charades for two words.

VOCABULARY FROM CLASSICAL ROOTS

ASSIGN WRITTEN EXERCISES

Exercise A: Matching (page 16)

1. C 2. D 3. A 4. E 5. F
6. B 7.–12. Sentences will vary.

Exercise B: Sorting (pages 16–18)

1. VIS	2. SPECT	3. AUDI	4. PHON	5. DICT	6. VOC-
envision	spectator	audible	saxophone	dictation	vocal
visible	prospect	inaudible	megaphone	dictator	vocalist
supervise	spectacle	audience	phonics	contradict	vocation
visor	spectacular	audition	symphony	predict	avocation
revise	respect	auditorium	stereophonic	verdict	
				addictive	

Answers will vary regarding the words that students add to the lists.

A. 4   B. 3   C. 1, 2, 4, 5   D. seeing   E. hearing   F. speaking

Exercise C: Vocabulary from Your Textbooks (page 18)

1. verdict   2. phonics   3. addictive   4. vocation   5. audible

Exercise D: Rhyming Riddles (pages 18–19)

1. B   2. D   3. A   4. C

Exercise E: Writing and Discussion Activities (pages 19–20)

Answers will vary.

LESSON 5: WRITING (PAGES 21–25)

> ### Key Words
>
> | | | | |
> |---|---|---|---|
> | autobiography | autograph | biography | geography |
> | paragraph | postscript | prescription | scribe |
> | script | subscription | | |

INTRODUCE LESSON 5

(page 21) Introduce Lesson 5 orally by having students read the title "Writing" and the two featured roots *scrib/scrip* and *graph*, both of which mean "written."

Tell students: In school you write by hand, but there are other ways of writing, or recording. How else is writing done? (Examples: Writing is done via keyboarding on a computer. When a person takes a lie detector test on a poly*graph*, the needle or stylus on the machine writes the results. In hospitals, the electrocardio*graph* writes, or graphs, the condition of the heart. Code breakers tran*scrib*e coded messages into written language we can understand.) Call students' attention to the *graph* and *scrib* roots in the italicized writing-related words.

PREVIEW FAMILIAR WORDS

(pages 21, 23) *describe, description, scribble, digraph, graph*

Activity 1: *scrib/scrip*

Display the familiar words *describe, description,* and *scribble*. Read them orally and then chorally with the class. Underline the root *scrib/scrip* in each one.

Ask students the following questions:

Which familiar word reminds you of what you did when you were first trying to do *written* work? (scribble)

Look at the familiar words *describe* and *description*. What are the differences in the spelling of the root and in the pronunciation of *describe* and *description*? (In *describe*, the root is spelled *scrib* and the letter *i* has a long sound. In *description*, the root is spelled *scrip*, and the letter *i* in the root has a short sound.) Point out that the same patterns of spelling and pronunciation will hold for the lesson's key words, *prescribe* (and *prescription*), *subscribe* (and *subscription*).

When you *write* a description of a person, what elements might you include? (details about the person's physical appearance, clothing, temperament, and so on)

Ask: What is the shared meaning for the root *scrib/scrip* in the words *describe, description,* and *scribble*? (writing or written)

Activity 2: *graph*

Display the familiar words *digraph* and *graph*. Read them orally and then chorally with the class. Underline the root *graph* in each one.

Ask students the following questions:

What kinds of graphs have you seen in your textbooks? (Examples: line graphs, bar graphs, picture graphs)

What connection is there between the root *graph*, meaning "to write," and the graphs that you have studied in other subjects? (Graphs present information that is *written* or printed or recorded with lines, bars, drawings, and so on.)

Which familiar word is a phonics term for two letters *written* together to stand for one sound, like *ph, ch, th, wh, ng* and *sh*? (*digraph*) Do you see a digraph in the word *digraph*? (yes, the *ph* at the end)

Ask: What is the shared meaning for the root *graph* in *digraph* and *graph*? (written or writing)

PRESENT KEY WORDS

Display the key words. Read them orally and then chorally with the class.

Have the students underline the root in each key word in the box on page 21; then have them check to be sure that their words look like this.

autobio<u>graphy</u>	auto<u>graph</u>	bio<u>graphy</u>	geo<u>graphy</u>
para<u>graph</u>	post<u>script</u>	pre<u>scrip</u>tion	<u>scribe</u>
<u>script</u>	sub<u>scrip</u>tion		

Ask students the following questions:

Which key words begin with a root? (*scribe* and *script*) These two words have only one letter beyond the root, and both words are nouns. They would fit correctly in this sentence: "The scribe wrote a script for a play." One is a person, and the other is a thing. Which is which? (A *scribe* is a person who writes. A *script* is a thing, a booklet of pages for a presentation.)

In which key words does *scrib/scrip* or *graph* <u>not</u> appear at the beginning? (*autobiography, autograph, biography, geography, paragraph, postscript, prescription, subscription*)

Eight of the ten words in this lesson have more than one meaningful part. You have already met, or you will meet, some of those meaningful parts in other lessons. But in Exercise C of this lesson, you will meet *auto* and *bio*. Which of those two Greek roots do you associate with the science of living things? (*bio* for biology)

As students complete the "Using Root Clues" section, encourage them to use the meanings of the roots to find the correct answer. Have them match the columns <u>before</u> they study the complete definitions of the words.

LESSON 5: WRITING

Dictate the answers so that students can check themselves.

(page 21) 1. C   2. A   3. D   4. B

Present each key word, paying attention to pronunciation, part of speech, definition with context sentence, and other parts of the listing as applicable (additional derivation, related word form, illustration).

The words *paragraph* and *geography* (page 23) have additional derivations. They start with Greek roots, which are defined in the first line of the entry. What science, in which we study rocks, starts with the same Greek root as *geography*? (geology)

The illustration that accompanies *geography* is a rough sketch of a continent. Which continent? (Australia)

There are related verb forms given for some of the key words that are nouns. Note that on page 22 at the end of the entry for *prescription* is "*prescribe*, v." At the end of the entry for *subscription* is "*subscribe*, v." Remind students of the changes in spelling and pronunciation.

On page 23, there are adjective forms (ending in the suffix *-ical*) included at the end of the entry for the nouns *autobiography* (*autobiographical*, adj.), *biography* (*biographical*, adj.), and *geography* (*geographical*, adj.). Have students make up sentences in which they use the adjective forms of these words.

GUIDE ORAL PRACTICE
Activity 1: Connections and Examples

Some of you have read *biographies* of famous people. But if a famous person writes a book, telling his or her own life story, it is not called a biography. What is it called? (an autobiography) Suppose a famous person signs his or her name on the title page of the book. Which of the key words names that signature? (autograph)

You met the prefix *pre-* in Lesson 3. What does it mean? (before) So, what is a *prescription*? (something "written before") Does a doctor write a prescription for medicine before or after you go to the pharmacy to get the medicine? (before)

The prefixes *pre-* and *post-* have opposite meanings, "before" and "after." In history books, you might read about "*pre*war" events and "*post*war" events. Which events happened after the war? (*postwar* events) Which key word starts with the prefix *post*? (*postscript*) When do you think a writer adds a *postscript* to a letter? (after writing the letter and signing it) Why would a writer add a postscript? (probably because of remembering something not mentioned in the letter)

Which key word do you connect with a topic sentence? (*paragraph*) When you are writing, what do you do to show that you are starting a new paragraph? (indent the first word)

Which key word do you connect with receiving a newspaper or a magazine regularly? (*subscription*) Do people have to pay for subscriptions? (yes) You might want to have a student find out from the librarian what some subscriptions cost.

Activity 2: Draw, Display, Discuss

Do any of you have *autographed* books, balls, or other items to display? (Have students show or describe these things to the class and tell about the person who signed the item.)

Let's make a class list of the *biographies* and *autobiographies* you have read. Where in the library do you find these books?

Some of the typefaces on the computer imitate the look of handwriting in cursive *script*. Have students find some examples on the computer. (Examples: Lucinda Handwriting, Lucinda Calligraphy, Vladimir Script, Freestyle Script, and so on.) Then ask them to type several sentences using some of these scripts.

In social studies, you learn the *geography* of many places on earth. Look at the maps in our classroom. What *geographical* features do they show? (Examples: boundary lines of states and nations, land elevations, climate, rainfall, capital cities, and so on)

ASSIGN WRITTEN EXERCISES

Exercise A: Synonyms (page 24)

1. a   2. d   3. d   4. b   5. c

Exercise B: Meaning in Context (page 24)

1. scripts   2. geography   3. biography   4. autobiography
5. scribe   6. paragraph

Exercise C: Extend Your Vocabulary (page 25)

1. biochemistry   2. biology   3. biosphere   4. automobile
5. automatic

Reproducible Worksheet: Lesson 5 (page 66 of this book)

LESSON 6: CONNECTING (PAGES 26–30)

> ## Key Words
>
> antisocial   association   commemorate   dissociate
>
> memento   memorandum   memorial   remembrance
>
> society   sociologist

INTRODUCE LESSON 6

(page 26) Introduce Lesson 6 orally by having students read the title "Connecting" and the two featured roots *soci* meaning "being part of a group," and *mem*, meaning "remembering."

Soci is the root of *as<u>soci</u>ating*, and associating (or connecting, relating, joining, linking) helps with re<u>mem</u>bering. One of the best ways to remember a new piece of information is to *associate* it with an old one. Ask students for examples of how they use associations to remember things at home, school, or in sports. (Answers will vary.)

PREVIEW FAMILIAR WORDS

(pages 26, 28) *associate, social, social studies, memory, remember*

Activity 1: *soci*

Display the familiar words *associate, social,* and *social studies.* Read them orally and then chorally with the class. Underline the root *soci* in each one.

Ask students the following questions:

What characteristics or qualities do you *associate* with our state, city, and school? (Through discussion, have students identify *associate* as a verb.)

If I ask you who your *associates* are, what are you telling me? (who you play sports with, who you study with, and so on) As you can see, *associate* can be a verb or a noun. Talk about the change in pronunciation for the verb and noun forms.

Tell students that *associate* is often used in the "social sense," when we mean *associating* in terms of mingling with *groups of people*. The familiar term, social studies, includes history, which emphasizes the *groups of people* whose stories make history. Who are the people you have recently learned about in social studies? (Answers will vary.)

Ask: What are the shared meanings for the root *soci* in the words *associate, social,* and *social studies*? (connecting, being part of a group of people)

Activity 2: *mem*

Display the familiar words *memory* and *remember*. Read them orally and then chorally with the class. Underline the root *mem* in each one.

Ask students the following questions:

In what ways do you honor the *memory* of people who lived before you; how do you *remember* significant events that took place in earlier times? (through days set apart for remembering and honoring people of the past, through visiting memorials for people who contributed to the world)

Ask: What is the shared meaning for the root *mem* in *memory* and *remember*? (remembering)

PRESENT KEY WORDS

Display the key words. Read them orally and then chorally with the class.

Have students underline the root in each key word in the box on page 26; then have them check to be sure that their words look like this.

anti<u>soc</u>ial	a<u>ssoc</u>iation	com<u>mem</u>orate	dis<u>soc</u>iate
<u>mem</u>ento	<u>mem</u>orandum	<u>mem</u>orial	re<u>mem</u>brance
<u>soc</u>iety	<u>soc</u>iologist		

Ask students the following questions:

Which key words begin with a root? (*memento, memorandum, memorial, society, sociologist*)

In which key words does the root <u>not</u> appear at the beginning? (*antisocial, association, commemorate, dissociate, remembrance*)

Look again at the five key words in which the root does not appear at the beginning. Which two of those words start with a prefix that changes the word it is attached to into its antonym? (*antisocial* and *dissociate*)

What meanings do these prefixes have? (They bring a negative meaning to the words on which they appear; for example, *antismoking* and *antislavery* mean "against smoking" and "against slavery." The words *dissatisfied* and *discontented* mean "not satisfied," the opposite of satisfied, and "not contented.")

Since to *associate* means "to connect," what do you think its antonym to *dissociate* means? (to disconnect, to do the opposite of connect, to separate)

The key word *sociologist* ends in a suffix you will meet in Exercise C. Can you associate *sociologist* with any other words you know that end in the same *-logist* suffix? (Examples: *biologist, geologist, zoologist*)

As students complete the "Using Root Clues" section, encourage them to use the meanings of the roots to find the correct answer. Have them match the columns <u>before</u> they study the complete definitions of the words.

Dictate answers so that students can check themselves.

LESSON 6: CONNECTING

(page 26) 1. B   2. D   3. A   4. C

Present each key word, paying attention to pronunciation, part of speech, definition with context sentence, and other parts of the listing as applicable (additional derivation, related word form, illustration).

The *Nota Bene* on page 27 on *association* and *society* points out that they can be synonyms. But note also that there are <u>two</u> noun definitions for both *association* and *society*, one of which differentiates each of them from the "club, organization" meaning.

GUIDE ORAL PRACTICE
Activity 1: Connections and Examples

The words *club, society, association,* and *organization* are synonyms. What are the names of some organizations, societies, or associations that you know? (Answers will vary.)

Memorials are built to *commemorate*, or in *remembrance* of, people and events. What memorials (statues, monuments) have you visited or seen in photographs? Who or what do they commemorate? (Answers will vary.)

Activity 2: Draw, Display, Discuss

Hold up a memo from the school office. Ask: What are memorandums for? (to remind people of some information) What is the short form of the word *memorandum*? (memo)

Have students bring some of their *mementos* of trips, special occasions, or celebrations to class to describe to their classmates.

If someone sends you a *remembrance* for your birthday, what do you receive? (gift or present)

ASSIGN WRITTEN EXERCISES
Exercise A: Synonyms (page 29)

1. a   2. c   3. b   4. c   5. d

Exercise B: Meaning in Context (page 29)

1. Association 2. commemorate 3. mementos 4. remembrance 5. Memorial

Exercise C: Extend Your Vocabulary (page 30)

1. biology   2. zoology   3. geology   4. psychology   5. paleontology
6. biologist 7. zoologist 8. geologist 9. B   10. A

Reproducible Worksheet: Lesson 6 (page 67 in this book)

LESSON 7: LOWERING (WITH PREFIXES) (PAGES 31–35)

> **Key Words**
>
> | | | | |
> |---|---|---|---|
> | decrease | dejected | demote | denominator |
> | descend | subdue | subheading | submerge |
> | subside | subsistence | | |

INTRODUCE LESSON 7

(page 31) Introduce Lesson 7 orally by having students read the title "Lowering (with Prefixes)" and the two featured prefixes *de-*, meaning "down," and *sub-*, meaning "under; below."

The idea of "lower" is a part of the meaning of both of these prefixes. When we <u>sub</u>tract, we make the first number go down; it becomes *lower.* When nature causes <u>de</u>struction, buildings are toppled, *lowered,* or brought down. As you study the words in this unit, look for the idea of "lower" in their meaning.

Nota Bene to teacher: Since this lesson is the first one in this book to focus primarily on prefixes, it provides a good opportunity to review the prefixes presented in the preceding book of the series, *Vocabulary from Classical Roots* 5.

bi- (two) as in bilingual

com-/con- (together) as in committee and conjunction

dis- (not) as in disagree

ex- (out) as in extract

in- (not) as in insignificant

inter- (between) as in interval

non- (not) as in nonfiction

quadr- (four) as in quadrilateral

re- (again) as in relate

semi- (partly) as in semiconscious

trans- (across) as in transact

tri- (three) as in triplet

un- (not) as in unlucky

uni- (one) as in unicycle

LESSON 7: LOWERING (WITH PREFIXES)

PREVIEW FAMILIAR WORDS

(pages 32, 33) *decline, defeat, destructive, submarine, subtract, subtraction, subway*

Activity 1: *de-*

Display the familiar words *decline, defeat,* and *destructive.* Read them orally and then chorally with the class. Underline the prefix *de-* in each one.

Ask students these questions:

Which familiar word makes you think of turning *down* an invitation? (*decline*)

Maybe you have heard the expression, "The thrill of victory, the agony of defeat." Why is defeat "agony"? (because the defeated player or team went *down* in the competition. It is painful to lose; for some, it is "agony.")

What do destructive storms do to trees? (knock them *down*)

Ask: What is the shared meaning for the prefix *de-* on the familiar words *decline, defeat,* and *destructive*? (down)

Activity 2: *sub-*

Display the familiar words *submarine, subtract, subtraction,* and *subway.*

Read them orally and then chorally with the class. Underline the prefix *sub-* in each one.

Ask students the following questions:

What is the location of a subway train? (*under*ground, downstairs *from* the street)

How is a submarine different from other ships? (It can go *under* water.)

When setting up a subtraction problem, where do you put the number you are subtracting? (*below* the other number)

Ask: What is the shared meaning for the prefix *sub-* in the familiar words *submarine, subtract, subtraction, subway*? (under; below)

PRESENT KEY WORDS

Display the key words. Read them orally and then chorally with the class.

Have students underline the root in each key word in the box on page 31; then have them check to be sure that their words look like this.

decrease	dejected	demote	denominator
descend	subdue	subheading	submerge
subside	subsistence		

Ask students the following questions:

There are ten key words in Lesson 7. How many begin with a prefix? (all ten)

VOCABULARY FROM CLASSICAL ROOTS

Often a base word (to which a prefix is added) provides an additional clue to the word's meaning.

For example, look at the word *subheading*. What is the main heading, or title, of this lesson? (Lesson 7: Lowering (with Prefixes)) What is one of the subheadings in this lesson? (Example: Using Prefix Clues)

Where is it located in relation to the lesson heading? (below it)

As students complete the "Using Prefix Clues" section, encourage them to use the meanings of the prefixes to find the correct answer. Have them match the columns <u>before</u> they study the complete definitions of the words.

Dictate answers so that students can check themselves.

(page 31) 1. C   2. D   3. A   4. B

Present each key word, paying attention to pronunciation, part of speech, definition with context sentence, and other parts of the listing as applicable (additional derivation, related word form, illustration).

Remind students that knowing a key word will help them understand its related forms. On pages 32 and 33, point out the related noun forms at the end of the entries for the verbs *demote* (*demotion*, n.), *descend* (*descent*, n.), and *submerge* (*submersion*, n.)

At the end of the entry for the noun *subsistence* is the related verb form *subsist*.

The words *decrease, dejected, demote, descent, submerge, subside,* and *subsistence* contain additional Latin derivations which contribute to their meanings. For each word, read the information within the brackets. Which word has a Latin root that means "to climb"? (*descend*, from *scandere*) Ask students to look at the illustration of the climbers. Are they ascending or descending the mountain? How do you know? (descending because they are looking below themselves for where to put their feet) Have students look at the dolphins. Which one is submerged? (the one in the foreground)

GUIDE ORAL PRACTICE

Activity 1: Connections and Examples

You may discover that you have associations with, or prior knowledge of, some of the key words. Using what you already know, answer these questions.

Which word leads you think of a fraction? (*denominator*)

Which word do you associate with a submarine? (*submerge*)

Which word do you associate with going downstairs? (*descend*)

Which key word is the opposite of *increase*? (*decrease*) If increasing is "making more," what is decreasing? (making less)

Which key word is the opposite of *promote*? (*demote*) If a promotion *raises* you, what does a demotion do? (lowers you)

LESSON 7: LOWERING (WITH PREFIXES)

When the drainpipe below your kitchen sink is clogged, the water in the sink drains slowly. It takes a long time for the level of the water to subside. In this context, what does *subside* mean? (get lower, go down)

Activity 2: Draw, Display, Discuss

Ask students what they know about the causes and effects of floods. Has anyone seen his/her own yard *submerged*? Where do people go as they wait for floodwaters to *subside* so that they can return to their homes? (to shelters, motels, homes of friends or relatives) How are the words *dejected* and *subdued* related to the experience of a flood? (Very often people have these feelings after a flood. They look downhearted. They speak quietly and sadly about all they have lost.)

Where have storms and floods reduced people to living on bare *subsistence*? (tsunami and earthquake regions) Do newborn babies need both food and drink for subsistence? (No, they can live on just milk.) Do all teenagers need the same amount of food and drink for subsistence? (No, people differ in the amounts of food and drink they need, just to stay alive.)

ASSIGN WRITTEN EXERCISES

Exercise A: Antonyms (page 34)

1. b   2. d   3. c   4. a   5. b

Exercise B: Meaning in Context (page 34)

1. subside   2. subdued   3. descend   4. submerged   5. decreased

Exercise C: Extend Your Vocabulary (pages 34–35)

1. proposal   2. propellers   3. protecting   4. provisions   5. projectile

Reproducible Worksheet: Lesson 7 (page 68 in this book)

VOCABULARY FROM CLASSICAL ROOTS

LESSON 8: REVIEWING LESSONS 5–7 (PAGES 36–40)

Before your students do the written review exercises in the book, conduct an oral review of the meanings of the featured roots and prefixes, the word parts introduced in each Exercise C, and the key vocabulary from Lessons 5, 6, and 7.

DISCUSS

Use these kinds of questions to challenge students.

What is the connection in meaning between the words *memorial* and *memento*? (They both have the *mem* root, which can mean "remember." *Memorials* help people remember an important person or event. *Mementos* help individuals remember times that are personally significant to them.) Lesson 6

Since *sub-* means "under," why doesn't *subside* mean "under the side"? (In the word *subside*, *side* is a root derived from Latin *sidere* meaning "to sink") Lesson 7

Both *subdued* and *dejected* suggest moods that are "down." But how are they different? Which one is stronger? (*dejected*, because it means "downhearted," while *subdued* may mean only "calm and quiet with feelings under control") Lesson 7

Think of a long word, meaning "written reminder," that can be shortened down to two syllables. (*memorandum* which can be shortened to *memo*) Lesson 6

Think of the two key words *scribe* and *script*, which are spelled almost the same as the *scrib/scrip* root. Are their meanings closely related to the meaning of the root? (Yes, they are. The root *scrib/scrip* comes from the Latin word for "write." *Scribe* is the word for a person who writes, and *script* is the word for something that has been written down.) Lesson 5

REINFORCE

Most words that end in *-logy/-logist* refer to sciences and scientists or specialists, as with *sociology/sociologist*. A specialist in hearing may be called an *audiologist*. What do you think the science of hearing is called? (audiology) Lesson 6

What is the shared meaning of *auto-* in the words *autograph* and *autobiography*? (self) What equipment should an autograph collector carry at all times? (a pen for people to use to write their signatures) Lesson 5

The word *biography* starts with *bio-*, which means "life." What is a biography you have read recently? What is a biography you would like to read? (Answers will vary.) Lesson 5

Bio- is combined often with words or roots connected with science. Use a dictionary to find several of these science words. Are any of them familiar? (Examples: *biology, bionics, biosphere, biofeedback, biodegradable*) Lesson 5

What words in this sentence have a prefix that means *forward*: I will provide you with a proposal for her promotion. (*provide, proposal, promotion*) Explain the "forward" connection for each word. (To provide is "to come forward with;" a proposal is a plan "put forward;" a promotion is a "move forward or upward.") Lesson 7

LESSON 8: REVIEWING LESSONS 5–7

EXPLORE

When students would benefit from a more in-depth exploration of a particular word, the additional word-learning strategies at the beginning of this book (pages vi–viii) can be helpful.

GUIDE ORAL PRACTICE

Activity 1: Definition Challenge

Give each student a card (3" by 5" or 5" by 7"). Assign each student one of the thirty words from the box at the top of page 37 in the student book. Have the student copy the complete definition of that word on the card. Line up the class in two teams, facing each other.

The first student on Team A reads a definition. The first student on Team B can earn two points by coming up with the word that fits the definition. If the answer is incorrect, Team B may still earn one point if another member can come up with the word.

The teams take turns until all the definitions have been read. The team with the most points wins.

Activity 2: Charades (sorting by parts of speech)

Hand each student another blank card (3" by 5" or 5" by 7"). Again assign to each student one of the thirty words, but make sure it is a different one from the word the student had for Activity 1. The student will copy the new word and its full definition from the book.

VOCABULARY FROM CLASSICAL ROOTS

Write these categories on the board: nouns, adjectives, verbs, two parts of speech. Have students sort themselves into these groups, according to the part of speech of their assigned words, and line up in alphabetical order. Their groupings should look like this.

Nouns	Adjectives	Verbs	Two Parts of Speech
association	antisocial	commemorate	autograph
autobiography	dejected	demote	decrease
biography		descend	memorial
denominator		dissociate	
geography		subdue	
memento		submerge	
memorandum		subside	
paragraph			
postscript			
prescription			
remembrance			
scribe			
script			
society			
sociologist			
subheading			
subscription			
subsistence			

Break the noun group in half, and combine all the other groups. You will then have three groups. Tell each group to select two of their words to act out, as in charades. Allow a little time for each group to plan the charades. All of the group's words should stay on display while the acting is taking place. The other students have to guess which word is being portrayed.

LESSON 8: REVIEWING LESSONS 5–7

Activity 3: Charades (sorting by syllables)

Have each student give his or her word card from the previous activity to another student. Tell students to sort themselves into new groups, according to the number of syllables in their word. Then, have each group line up in alphabetical order, while holding up their cards. Their groupings should look like this.

One	Two	Three	Four	Five	Six
scribe	decrease	autograph	antisocial	association	autobiography
script	demote	dejected	biography	denominator	
	descend	memento	commemorate	sociologist	
	postscript	paragraph	dissociate		
	subdue	prescription	geography		
	submerge	remembrance	memorandum		
	subside	subheading	memorial		
		subscription	society		
		subsistence			

Reduce to three groups by having the five-syllable and six-syllable words join the four-syllable group, and by having the two one-syllable words join the two-syllable group.

Proceed as above, with each group planning charades for two words.

ASSIGN WRITTEN EXERCISES
Exercise A: Matching (page 36)

1. B 2. C 3. G 4. A 5. H
6. I 7. D 8. F 9. E
10.–12. Sentences will vary.

Exercise B: Sorting (pages 37–38)

1. SCRIB/SCRIP	2. GRAPH	3. MEM
script	autograph	remembrance
postscript	autobiography	memorial
scribe	geography	memento
prescription	biography	memorandum
subscription	paragraph	commemorate

4. SOCI	**5. DE-**	**6. SUB-**
association	decrease	subsistence
sociologist	descend	subside
society	denominator	submerge
antisocial	dejected	subdue
dissociate	demote	subheading

Answers will vary regarding the words that students add to the lists.

A. 4 B. 2 C. 3 D. 2
E. subscription F. writing G. lowering

Exercise C: Vocabulary from Your Textbooks (page 38)

1. geography 2. prescription 3. denominator 4. subheading 5. memorial

Exercise D: Rhyming Riddles (page 39)

1. C 2. E 3. B 4. A 5. D

Exercise E: Writing and Discussion Activities (pages 39–40)

Answers will vary.

LESSON 9: SENDING (PAGES 41–45)

> **Key Words**
>
> admit   deportation   emit   missile
> mission   omit   portable   portfolio
> rapport   submit

INTRODUCE LESSON 9

(page 41) Introduce Lesson 9 orally by having students read the title "Sending" and the two featured roots *port*, meaning "carry," and *mis/mit*, meaning "send."

What connection do you see between "carrying" and "sending"? (Both involve moving something from one place or person to another.)

PREVIEW FAMILIAR WORDS

(pages 41, 42) *port, export, import, missionary, dismiss, transmit*

Activity 1: *port*

Display the familiar words *port, export,* and *import*. Read them orally and then chorally with the class. Underline the root *port* in each one.

Ask students the following questions:

Remind students that *port* is a word as well as a root. What are some large cities that have important shipping ports? (Accept the names of any coastline cities with a harbor.) What do the ships using these ports *carry*? (Answers will vary. Examples: cars, oil, food, manufactured goods, passengers)

On the words *import* and *export,* what do the prefixes mean? (*im-* means "in," and *ex-* means "out.") What are some things this country imports? What things does this country export? (Answers will vary.)

Ask: What is the shared meaning for the root *port* in the familiar words *port, import,* and *export*? (carry)

Activity 2: *mis/mit*

Display the familiar words *missionary, dismiss, transmit*. Read them orally and then chorally with the class. Underline the root *mis* or *mit* in each one.

Ask students the following questions:

What do the two parts of *transmit* mean? (*Trans* means "across," and *mit* means "send," so *transmit* means "send across.") On a computer, how do you transmit e-mail? (You click on "send.")

When your teacher dismisses your class from school, what happens? (All the students leave; they are *sent* away from school.)

Missionaries are people who go to other countries to teach their religion. What connection is there between the root *mis* and the meaning of the word missionary? (A missionary is usually *sent* to some place to do the teaching work.)

Ask: What is the shared meaning for the root *mis/mit* in the familiar words *missionary, dismiss, transmit?* (send or sent)

PRESENT KEY WORDS

Display the key words. Read them orally and then chorally with the class.

Have students underline the root in each key word in the box on page 41; then have them check to be sure that their words look like this.

ad<u>mit</u>	dep<u>or</u>tation	e<u>mit</u>	<u>miss</u>ile
<u>miss</u>ion	o<u>mit</u>	<u>por</u>table	<u>por</u>tfolio
rap<u>or</u>t	sub<u>mit</u>		

Which words begin with a root? (*missile, mission, portable, portfolio*)

Among the words in which the root does *not* appear at the beginning, there are some that start with familiar prefixes. Which one starts with a prefix that means "under"? (submit) So, the parts of the word *submit* give you clues that suggest "to send under." This is not a complete definition, of course. Roots lead you in the direction of the meaning but do not always give you a full definition of a word.)

You have seen the prefix *ad-* before, in the word *addictive*. What does the prefix *ad-* mean? ("to" or "toward") So, what does *admit* mean? ("to send to" or "toward") When you are *admitted* to the movies, are you "sent toward" the seats? (yes)

As students complete the "Using Root Clues" section, encourage them to use the meanings of the roots to find the correct answer. Have them match the columns <u>before</u> they study the complete definitions of the words.

Dictate the answers so that students can check themselves.

(page 41) 1. D   2. C   3. A   4. B

Present each key word, paying attention to pronunciation, part of speech, definition with context sentence, and other parts of the listing as applicable (additional derivation, related word form, illustration).

On page 43 are two noun definitions of *mission* and two verb definitions of *submit*. Which definition of *mission* would fit the mission of our school? (the first) Which definition of *submit* would fit an author mailing a manuscript to a publisher? (the second)

Remind students that knowing a key word will help them understand its related

LESSON 9: SENDING

forms. On pages 42–43, related noun forms are included for these *mis/mit* verbs: *admit* (*admission*, n.), *emit* (*emission*, n.), *omit* (*omission*, n.), *submit* (*submission*, n.). Exercise C addresses these key words and their related forms.

GUIDE ORAL PRACTICE
Activity 1: Connections and Examples

What is the meaning of the prefix *e-* or *ex-*? (out) What does *emit* mean? (send out)

In traffic, when have you seen or smelled *emissions*? (when following a vehicle whose tailpipe is pouring out black smoke) Why are *emissions* a problem? (The gases pollute the air we breathe.)

Today's *missiles* are often guided by computers. But that was not always the case. Over the years, what other kinds of missiles have been used? (Examples: stones that were catapulted, cannonballs that were fired)

Activity 2: Draw, Display, Discuss

What *portable* equipment do you think would be useful to organizations that are carrying out rescue or aid *missions* in remote areas? (Examples: battery-operated cell phones, tents, medicines, food packs, and so on.)

Draw a picture that shows people who do not feel *rapport* with each other. (Drawings will vary but will show people in disagreement with each other.)

Both *deportation* and *exportation* involve going out of or away from a country. What is the difference between them? (*Deportation* is sending people out of a country because they broke certain laws. *Exportation* is sending things out of a country to sell them.)

Suppose you are asked to turn in a *portfolio* of your best work in English class. List three papers you would include in the portfolio and one that you would omit. Explain your choices. (Answers will vary.)

ASSIGN WRITTEN EXERCISES
Exercise A: Synonyms (pages 43–44)

1. c 2. d 3. d 4. b 5. a

Exercise B: Meaning in Context (page 44)

1. emitting 2. admit 3. omit 4. submit 5. mission

Exercise C: Extend Your Vocabulary (pages 44–45)

1. remission 2. commission 3. permission 4. transmission 5. admission
6. submission 7. transmit 8. permit 9. verbs 10. nouns

Reproducible Worksheet: Lesson 9 (page 69 in this book)

VOCABULARY FROM CLASSICAL ROOTS

LESSON 10: TURNING (PAGES 46–50)

Key Words

contradictory	contrary	contrast	controversial
divert	reverse	versatile	version
versus	vertebrate		

INTRODUCE LESSON 10

(page 46) Introduce Lesson 10 orally by having students read the title "Turning" and the two featured roots *vers/vert*, meaning "to turn," and *contra*, meaning "against."

Have students consider how these roots are related. Ask: Do you like going to parks for picnics and games? (yes) But suppose the city wanted to build a park on the land where you live. Would you "turn toward" or "turn against" that idea? (Probably the majority would "turn against.") So the proposed park would become a subject for argument and debate; it would become a *controversial* topic on which two sides "turn against" each other. Do you hear the two roots from this lesson in the word *controversial*? (yes)

Nota Bene to teacher: In this part of the oral introduction to the lesson, deal with the word *controversial* only orally, as the connection between the two roots. In the next part of the introduction, you will call attention to the variance in spelling: *contro* rather than *contra*.

PREVIEW FAMILIAR WORDS

(pages 47, 48) *adversary, advertise, invert, contradict, contradiction*

Activity 1: vers/vert

Display the familiar words *adversary, advertise,* and *invert*. Read them orally and then chorally with the class. Underline the root *vers/vert* in each one.

Ask students the following questions:

When you *invert* a fraction, what do you do to it? (You *turn* it upside down.)

The familiar words *adversary* and *advertise* start with the same letters, and they share a root, but they are very different in meaning.

Which word do you associate with "turning toward" buying something? (*advertise*)

Which word do you associate with "turning toward" a person who is your opponent? (*adversary*) A gymnast might call someone whom he respects as a competitor "a worthy *adversary*." But in any adversarial relationship, the people are opponents. Which schools are our *adversaries* in sports? (Answers will vary.)

LESSON 10: TURNING

Ask: What is the shared meaning for the root *vers/vert* in the words *adversary, advertise,* and *invert*? (turning)

Activity 2: *contra*

Display the familiar words *contradict* and *contradiction*. Read them orally and then chorally with the class. Underline *contra* in each one.

Ask students the following questions:

Do you remember the meaning of the root *dict*, which we studied in Lesson 3? (to say or speak) When you *contradict* someone, what are you doing? (You are "speaking against" whatever that person said.)

A contradiction is a statement "against," a denial of what a person said. If I said, "The planet closest to the sun is Jupiter," I would expect you to contradict me. What would you say in *contradiction* to my incorrect statement? (No, the planet closest to the sun is *not* Jupiter. It is Mercury.)

Ask: What is the meaning for the root *contra* in *contradict* and *contradiction*? (against)

PRESENT KEY WORDS

Display the key words. Read them orally and then chorally with the class.

Have students underline the root in each key word in the box on page 46; then have them check to be sure that their words look like this.

contra<u>dict</u>ory	cont<u>rar</u>y	cont<u>r</u>ast	cont<u>ro</u>versial
di<u>vert</u>	re<u>vers</u>e	<u>vers</u>atile	<u>vers</u>ion
<u>vers</u>us	<u>vert</u>ebrate		

Which key words start with *contra* or *vers/vert*? (*contradictory, contrary, contrast, versatile, version, versus, vertebrate*)

Sometimes the root *contra* is spelled with a different last vowel, the vowel <u>o</u>. In which key word do you see this variance in spelling? (*controversial*)

What are the two clues to meaning in the two roots of the word *controversial*? (*Contra/o* means "against" and *vers* means "turning.")

Look at the key words *divert* and *reverse*. What prefixes do you see on those two words? (*di-* on *divert*, and *re-* on *reverse*) You will learn about the prefix *di-* in Exercise C of this lesson, but you probably already know the meaning of the prefix *re-*. What does it mean? (back or again)

As students complete the "Using Root Clues" section, encourage them to use the meanings of the roots to find the correct answer. Have them match the columns <u>before</u> they study the complete definitions of the words.

Dictate the answers so that students can check themselves.

(page 46) 1. B   2. A   3. D   4. C

Present each key word, paying attention to pronunciation, part of speech, definition with context sentence, and other parts of the listing as applicable (additional derivation, related word form, illustration).

This lesson offers good opportunities for students to practice with the multiple meanings of words. On pages 47 and 48, there are two verb definitions of *divert*, both an adjective and a verb definition for *reverse,* two preposition definitions of *versus,* and both a noun and a verb definition of *contrast*. Ask questions, such as the following, that alert students to the different meanings.

Which meaning of *divert* could be connected with a detour sign? (first)

Which meaning of *reverse* is more closely connected with a change of mind? (second)

Look at the abbreviation for *versus* and talk about when it is used.

Remind students that knowing a key word will help them understand its related forms. On pages 47 and 49, point out the related noun forms of *divert* (*diversion*, n.), *versatile* (*versatility*, n.), and *controversial* (*controversy*, n.). Have students use the related forms in sentences.

GUIDE ORAL PRACTICE
Activity 1: Connections and Examples

In science, students will have studied *vertebrates* and invertebrates. Draw a Venn diagram on the board. Label one circle *vertebrate* and the other *invertebrate*. Elicit from students the qualities for each category and the qualities that they have in common.

Ask students where the contrasting qualities of the two groups have been placed. (in the parts of the circles that do not overlap)

Name some vertebrates. (Examples: dogs, cats, fish)

Name some invertebrates. (Examples: ants, beetles, spiders)

How is the *vert* root, meaning "to turn," related to a vertebrate? (Vertebrates are flexible creatures; they are able to turn in different directions because their backbone of many joined parts allows them movement.)

How does the root meaning "turn" relate to a new *version* of an old story? (The story is given a new direction, or turn, while still remaining similar to the original.)

Why are some subjects *controversial*? (because they are topics about which people have opposing opinions)

Why do you hear *contradictory* opinions when you listen to a discussion of a controversial subject? (because people do not agree and speak against what another person has said)

What is the root of the word *versus*? (*vers*, which means "turning") What do we mean when we speak of one team *versus* another? (The teams are playing against one another.)

LESSON 10: TURNING

Activity 2: Draw, Display, Discuss

Maybe you first met the key word *contrary* in a nursery rhyme. Can anyone recite the rhyme in which *contrary* appears? (Mary, Mary, quite contrary, how does your garden grow?) If you can think back to the pictures of Mary, was she smiling or frowning? (Frowning. She was contrary, hard to please, probably against gardening.)

Draw several pictures to illustrate a versatile person. (Pictures may show a person cooking, swimming, playing an instrument, and so on.)

Ask students to bring in pictures of vertebrates and invertebrates. Then have the class sort them into the two categories.

ASSIGN WRITTEN EXERCISES
Exercise A: Antonyms (page 49)

1. a   2. c   3. b   4. a   5. d

Exercise B: Meaning in Context (page 49)

1. version   2. controversial   3. contradictory   4. contrary   5. divert

Exercise C: Extend Your Vocabulary (page 50)

di–a prefix	*di*–not a prefix
divide	dime
diversity	dishes
divorce	dipper
direction	dining
division	dirty

Reproducible Worksheet: Lesson 10 (page 70 in this book)

VOCABULARY FROM CLASSICAL ROOTS

LESSON 11: HANDLING (PAGES 51–55)

Key Words

commander	dissolve	management	maneuver
manicure	manual	manuscript	soluble
solution	solvent		

INTRODUCE LESSON 11

(page 51) Introduce Lesson 11 orally by having students read the title "Handling" and the two featured roots *man*, meaning "handle" or "use hands," and *sol/solv*, meaning "loosen; to release." Ask students how *managing* and *solving* are connected when they work on a jigsaw puzzle. (To find the solution, they need to handle the pieces and organize them in different ways to have the solution come about or be released.)

PREVIEW FAMILIAR WORDS

(pages 51, 53) *manage, manager, manufacture, solve*

Activity 1: *man*

Display the familiar words *manage, manager, manufacture*. Read them orally and then chorally with the class. Underline the root *man* in each one.

Ask students these questions:

Which familiar word names a person who is in charge of a store? (manager)

What does a *manager* do? (A manager *handles* or directs the operation of the business.)

What is the difference between a product that has been *manufactured* and a product that has been grown? (One is made by hand or by hands operating machines or using tools and one is made by nature.)

Ask: What is the shared meaning for the root *man* in *manage, manager,* and *manufacture*? (to handle or to use the hands)

Activity 2: *sol/solv*

Display the familiar word *solve*. Read it orally and then chorally with the class. Underline the root *solv* in it.

Ask: What is the connection in meaning between "solving" a problem and the root *solv* which means "to loosen, to release"? (When a person solves a problem, it is like undoing or loosening parts until the answer is released.)

LESSON 11: HANDLING

PRESENT KEY WORDS

Display the key words. Read them orally and then chorally with the class.

Have students underline the root in each key word in the box on page 51; then have them check to be sure that their words look like this.

com<u>man</u>der   dis<u>solv</u>e   <u>man</u>agement   <u>man</u>euver

<u>man</u>icure   <u>man</u>ual   <u>man</u>uscript   <u>solu</u>ble

<u>solu</u>tion   <u>solv</u>ent

There are ten key words in Lesson 11. How many begin with a root? (eight)

What prefixes do you see on the other two key words? (*com-* on *commander* and *dis-* on *dissolve*)

What does the prefix *com-* mean? (together) What is a *commander* doing as he directs his troops through various maneuvers? (He is managing them.)

What does the prefix *dis-* mean? (aside or apart) Can you predict what the meaning of *dissolve* might be? (something that loosens apart from itself)

As students complete the "Using Root Clues" section, encourage them to use the meanings of the roots to find the correct answer. Have them match the columns <u>before</u> they study the complete definitions of the words.

Dictate the answers so that students can check themselves.

(page 51) 1. B   2. D   3. A   4. C

Present each key word, paying attention to pronunciation, part of speech, definition with context sentence, and other parts of the listing as applicable (additional derivation, related word form, illustration).

Most of the words on pages 52 and 53 have two definitions. The words *management* and *solution* have two noun definitions each. *Dissolve* has two verb definitions. *Maneuver* and *manicure* have both noun and verb definitions. *Manual* and *manuscript* have both adjective and noun definitions. Ask questions such as the following to help students discriminate between the different meanings of each word.

Which definition of *dissolve* is <u>not</u> connected with liquids? (the second)

Which definition of *solution* is connected with liquids? (the second)

Draw students' attention to the additional derivation for the word *manicure*—the Latin *cura*, meaning "care." Ask them what other words do they associate with *cura* meaning "care"? (Examples: curable, curative, pedicure, a museum curator)

GUIDE ORAL PRACTICE

Activity 1: Connections and Examples

Explain that sometimes there is a strong literal connection between the meaning of a word and the meaning of its root. The connection is very easy to see. Other times the

VOCABULARY FROM CLASSICAL ROOTS

connection is not as literal, so it is not as easy to see. Which word—*maneuver* or *manicure*—has the more literal connection with the "hand" meaning of *man*? (Manicure is more literal because it is a treatment and care of the nails of the hands. To maneuver is to manage something in a skillful way. This is less directly connected to actual hands.)

Activity 2: Draw, Display, Discuss

What ingredients do you need to make an aqueous *solution*? (water and salt, sugar, food coloring, or any other *soluble* material that will *dissolve* in water)

Display a clear plastic or glass container with water. Have students select from an assortment of soluble and insoluble materials to add to the container. Observe which are soluble and which are not. (Examples: sugar, salt, staples, beads, and so on)

When you solve a math problem, you get the answer. Which key word is a synonym for *answer* in the math context? (*solution*)

What are some *solvents* you have at home? (paint removers, furniture stripping materials, fingernail polish remover) Why do you need to be careful when using these materials? (They are usually flammable and they often are made of chemicals that are not good to breathe.)

ASSIGN WRITTEN EXERCISES

Exercise A: Synonyms (page 54)

1. c 2. a 3. b 4. d 5. b

Exercise B: Meaning in Context (pages 54–55)

1. manual 2. management 3. dissolved 4. soluble 5. solution

Exercise C: Extend Your Vocabulary (page 55)

1. E 2. A 3. F 4. C
5. B 6. H 7. D 8. G
9. biped, quadruped, centipede   10. impede, expedition

Reproducible Worksheet: Lesson 11 (page 71 in the book)

LESSON 12: REVIEWING LESSONS 9–11 (PAGES 56–59)

Before your students do the written review exercises in the book, conduct an oral review of the meanings of the featured roots and prefixes, the word parts introduced in each Exercise C, and the key vocabulary from Lessons 9, 10, and 11.

DISCUSS

Use these kinds of questions to challenge students.

What is the connection in meaning between the words *reverse* and *controversial?* (They both have the *vers* root, which can mean "turn"; *reverse* means "turn back," and *controversial* means "turning against.") Lesson 10

How are *manicure* and *pedicure* related? (They share a Latin root that means "care of" and they have additional meaningful parts that mean "hand" (*man*) and "foot" (*ped*). Also they both result in well-trimmed nails.) Lesson 11

Man is a word meaning "adult male." The same three letters *man* can also be a root, meaning "hands, handling, managing." Does there seem to be any connection between the meaning of the base word and the root? (No. Explain to students that this is one case where there is no connection. The base word *man* is derived from Old English, not Latin.) Lesson 11

Port, which is a root meaning "carry," is also a word that means "harbor." What connection do you see between the word *port*, meaning "harbor" and the root *port*, meaning "carry"? (Ships go to *ports* to rest. The purpose of ships is *to carry* things.) What other roots and prefixes can you think of that are also words? (*graph*—written; *meter*—measurement; *super*—bigger; *in*—inward) Lesson 9

REINFORCE

What are some of the number prefixes that you can use with the root *ped* to name various creatures? (biped, quadruped, millipede, and so on) Lesson 11

Think of a two-syllable verb that means "turn aside." (*divert*) What part of that word is the "aside" prefix? (*di-*) What is another meaning of the prefix *di-?* (apart) What is the alternate spelling of the prefix *di-?* (*dis-* as in dissolve) How come *dis-* can also mean "not" as in *dislike* and *disagree?* (Prefixes, like words, can have multiple meanings.) Lesson 10

The suffix *-ion* appears on many words. When this suffix is added to a word that ends in the root *mit* (like *admit*), how does the spelling change? (The final *t* becomes *ss* before *-ion*: *admit* becomes *admission.*) Lesson 9

EXPLORE

When students would benefit from a more in-depth exploration of a particular word, the additional word-learning strategies at the beginning of this book (pages vi–viii) can be helpful.

VOCABULARY FROM CLASSICAL ROOTS

GUIDE ORAL PRACTICE

Activity 1: Definition Challenge

Give each student a card (3" by 5" or 5" by 7"). Assign each student one of the thirty words from the box at the top of page 57 in the student book. Have the student copy the complete definition of that word on the card. Line up the class in two teams, facing each other.

The first student on Team A reads a definition. The first student on Team B can earn two points by coming up with the word that fits the definition. If the answer is incorrect, Team B may still earn one point if another member can come up with the word.

The teams take turns until all the definitions have been read. The team with the most points wins.

Activity 2: Charades (sorting by parts of speech)

Hand each student another blank card (3" by 5" or 5" by 7"). Again assign to each student one of the thirty words, but make sure it is a different one from the word the student had for Activity 1. The student will copy the new word and its full definition from the book.

Write these categories on the board: nouns, verbs, adjectives, preposition, and two parts of speech. Have students sort themselves into these groups, according to the part of speech of their assigned words. Their groupings should look like this.

Nouns	Verbs	Adjectives	Preposition	Two Parts of Speech
commander	admit	contradictory	versus	contrast
deportation	dissolve	contrary		maneuver
management	divert	controversial		manicure
missile	emit	portable		manuscript
mission	omit	soluble		manual
portfolio	submit	versatile		reverse
rapport				
solution				
solvent				
version				
vertebrate				

Split the noun group in half, and have the one preposition join the smaller half. You will then have five groups of six students each. Tell each group to select two of their words to act out, as in charades. Allow a little time for each group to plan the charades. All of the group's words should stay on display while the acting is taking place. The other students have to guess which word is being portrayed.

LESSON 12: REVIEWING LESSONS 9–11

Activity 3: Charades (sorting by syllables)

Have each student give his or her word card from the previous activity to another student. Tell students to sort themselves into new groups, according to the number of syllables in their assigned words. Then have each group line up in alphabetical order, while holding up their cards. Their groupings should look like this:

Two	**Three**	**Four**	**Five**
admit	commander	controversial	contradictory
contrast	contrary	deportation	
dissolve	management	portfolio	
divert	maneuver		
emit	manicure		
missile	manual		
mission	manuscript		
omit	portable		
rapport	soluble		
reverse	solution		
solvent	versatile		
submit	vertebrate		
version			
versus			

Have students with two-syllable words form one group and students with the remaining words form a second group. Proceed as above, with each group planning charades for two words.

ASSIGN WRITTEN EXERCISES

Exercise A: Matching (page 56)

1. B   2. G   3. E   4. A

5. H   6. C   7. D   8. F

9.–12. Sentences will vary.

VOCABULARY FROM CLASSICAL ROOTS

Exercise B: Sorting (pages 57–58)

1. SOL/SOLV	2. MAN	3. VERS/VERT
solution	management	versus
dissolve	manual	vertebrate
solvent	maneuver	divert
soluble	manuscript	reverse
	manicure	versatile
	commander	version

4. CONTRA	5. PORT	6. MIS/MIT
contrast	deportation	mission
contrary	portable	submit
contradictory	portfolio	admit
controversial	rapport	emit
		missile
		omit

Answers will vary regarding the words that students add to the lists.

A. 1   B. 6   C. 3   D. *controversial*

Exercise C: Vocabulary from Your Textbooks (page 58)

1. soluble   2. vertebrate   3. missile   4. maneuver

Exercise D: Rhyming Riddles (page 58)

1. E   2. D   3. A   4. C   5. B

Exercise E: Writing and Discussion Activities (page 59)

Answers will vary.

LESSON 13: BELONGING (PAGES 60–64)

> ## Key Words
>
> cosmopolitan gene generation generosity
> international metropolitan nationality naturalize
> policy politician

INTRODUCE LESSON 13

(page 60) Introduce Lesson 13 orally by having students read the title "Belonging" and the three featured roots *poli,* meaning "city" or "citizen," *gen,* meaning "family," "race," or "birth," and *nat,* meaning "birthplace; born."

Ask students to think of different groups they belong to or are part of, beginning with their family. Have them think about sports teams, school clubs, community and religious organizations, their state and country. Ask them to draw circles to show the interrelationship (overlapping, separation, inclusion) of these different groups.

PREVIEW FAMILIAR WORDS

(pages 61, 62) *police, political, politics, general, gentle, nation, nature, native, natural*

Activity 1: *poli*

Display the familiar words *police, political,* and *politics.* Read them orally and then chorally with the class. Underline the root *poli* in each one.

Ask students the following questions:

What are your experiences with the *politics* of city, state, and national elections? (Answers will vary. Examples: yard signs for candidates, maybe going with parents to hand out campaign literature) What kind of work are *political* candidates competing to do? (the work of government, in the country, state, or city) Who decides which *political* candidate will get the job? (the citizens, by voting)

What part of the government do the *police* work for? (They are employed by cities to protect the citizens.) Who sets the salaries of the *police*? (elected and appointed officials of the government)

Ask: What is the shared meaning for the root *poli* in the words *police, political,* and *politics*? (city; citizen)

Activity 2: *gen*

Display the familiar words *general* and *gentle.* Read them orally and then chorally with the class. Underline the root *gen* in each one.

The root *gen* has a range of meanings. In which familiar word is its meaning related to being kind? (*gentle. Gentle* once had the meaning of being born to a good family. Such a person did not act harshly toward others.)

In the familiar word *general*, the meaning of *gen* is related to a group and to what is characteristic of the entire group. What are some general characteristics of students in this class? (similar age, hometown, and so on)

Ask: What is the shared meaning for the root *gen* in *general* and *gentle*? (family; group)

Activity 3: *nat*

Display the familiar words *nation, nature, native, natural*. Read them orally and then chorally with the class. Underline the root *nat* in each one.

Ask students the following questions:

Who are the members of the United *Nations*? (different countries or nations from all over the world)

Are you *native* to this area? (Answers will vary. Talk about the idea of being *born* in a place.) What are some plants that are not *native* to our region? (Answers will vary depending on climate.)

What do you enjoy about *nature*? (Answers will vary, but may include enjoying the changes in seasons, different aspects of nature such as mountains, coastal lands, and so on) What are some of the *natural* beauties of our region of the country? (Answers will vary.)

Ask: What is the shared meaning for the root *nat* in *nation, nature, native, natural*? (birthplace; born)

PRESENT KEY WORDS

Display the key words. Read them orally and then chorally with the class.

Have students underline the root in each key word in the box on page 60; then have them check to be sure that their words look like this.

cosmo<u>pol</u>itan	<u>gen</u>e	<u>gen</u>eration	<u>gen</u>erosity
inter<u>nat</u>ional	metro<u>pol</u>itan	<u>nat</u>ionality	<u>nat</u>uralize
<u>pol</u>icy	<u>pol</u>itician		

Which words begin with a root? (*gene, generation, generosity, nationality, naturalize, policy, politician*)

In which words does the root *not* appear at the beginning? (*cosmopolitan, international, metropolitan*)

Look at these meanings for the prefixes and see if they help you better understand and remember the meanings of the words. *Comso* comes from the Greek word *kosmos*, meaning "universe"; *inter* means "between."

LESSON 13: BELONGING

As students complete the "Using Root Clues" section, encourage them to use the meanings of the roots to find the correct answer. Have them match the columns <u>before</u> they study the complete definitions of the words.

Dictate answers so that students can check themselves.

(page 60) 1. D   2. A   3. B   4. C

Present each key word, paying attention to pronunciation, part of speech, definition with context sentence, and other parts of the listing as applicable (additional derivation, related word form, illustration).

Help students identify the illustration at the bottom of page 62 as the Eiffel Tower in Paris, France.

The *Nota Benes* on pages 62 and 63 lend themselves easily to word webs. In fact, the example of a word web on page vi in the front matter demonstrates several groups of words related to the *gen* root. Help your students make webs that show groups of words related to the roots *poli* and *nat*.

GUIDE ORAL PRACTICE
Activity 1: Connections and Examples

Remind students of the three levels of government—city, state, and national. Ask them to name some *politicians* who have been elected to office at each level. (Answers will vary. Try to elicit the president, vice president, and maybe a senator, representative, governor, mayor.)

If you had to tell a new student about our school *policies*, what would you say? (Examples: policies about absences, lateness, lunch arrangements, discipline, dress code)

Activity 2: Draw, Display, Discuss

Ask: How many *generations* of your family do you know? Grandparents? Great uncles or aunts? The "next generation," if a big sister or brother already has a baby? Show students how to draw a family tree. Have them start with their grandparents. Display their drawings in the classroom and have them make comparisons and contrasts.

Your parents and grandparents may have been born in this country, but perhaps they came from another country. As you trace your family tree back through the generations, how many *nationalities* do your ancestors represent?

Has anyone in your family become a *naturalized* citizen? Ask such students to tell a little about what steps the person took to do this and what the ceremony was like.

Where does *generosity* come from? Are we taught this or is it something in our *genes*? (Answers will vary. Encourage students to recall their behavior as young children as they discuss this.)

VOCABULARY FROM CLASSICAL ROOTS

ASSIGN WRITTEN EXERCISES

Exercise A: Synonyms (page 63)
1. c   2. c   3. d   4. a   5. b

Exercise B: Meaning in Context (page 64)
1. politician   2. generations   3. nationalities   4. naturalized   5. international

Exercise C: Extend Your Vocabulary (page 64)
1. music   2. beauty   3. magic   4. statistics   5. optics
6. biographer   7. conductor   8. spectator   9. subscriber   10. governor

Reproducible Worksheet: Lesson 13 (page 72 in this book)

LESSON 14: ILLUMINATING (PAGES 65–68)

> **Key Words**
>
> flamingo flammable inflammation inspire
> perspire photogenic photosynthesis respiration
> spirited telephoto

INTRODUCE LESSON 14

(page 65) Introduce Lesson 14 orally by having students read the title "Illuminating" and the three featured roots, *spir* meaning "breath; alive," *photo*, meaning "light," and *flam*, meaning "fire."

In cartoons, a character is sometimes shown with a lightbulb in a balloon overhead. What does the lightbulb signify? (an idea, an inspiration, or an understanding in the character's mind; a light has dawned)

When we say the "light of an idea dawns," are we using the word *light* figuratively or literally? (It is used figuratively. Literal "lighting" is closer to the illumination given by the flames of a fire.)

The roots *spir*, *photo*, and *flam* come together in the lesson title, "Illuminating," since illuminating can mean "lighting up," either figuratively or literally.

PREVIEW FAMILIAR WORDS

(pages 65, 66, 67) *spirit, photocopy, photograph, photographer, flame, inflame*

Activity 1: *spir*

Display the familiar word *spirit*. Read it orally and then chorally with the class. Underline the root *spir*.

Ask students the following questions:

When you are in good *spirits*, how do you feel? (happy, lively, very much alive)

Ask: What is the meaning for the root *spir* in the word *spirit*? (alive)

Activity 2: *photo*

Display the familiar words *photocopy, photograph,* and *photographer.* Read them orally and then chorally with the class. Underline the root *photo* in each one.

Ask students the following questions:

What is the short form for the word *photograph*? (*photo*)

VOCABULARY FROM CLASSICAL ROOTS

Is *photo* a word as well as a root? (yes) What does it mean? (A photo is a picture taken with a camera.)

Have any of you made *photocopies* on a copy machine? (Answers will vary.) Where can you make *photocopies*? (most libraries, the post office, a business that specializes in this work) What part does light play in the process of making *photocopies*? (When you place the page to be copied on a flat glass, the machine uses the interaction between light and electrically charged particles to make the copy.)

The word *photograph* comes from roots that mean "light" and "write." How is a photograph a "writing with light"? (Film is constructed in a way to record or "write" the image being captured by the amount of light that reaches the film.)

A *photographer* is a person who uses light to make a picture. What are some other words ending in *-er* or *-or* that name a person doing a particular job? (*teacher, farmer, surveyor,* and so on)

Ask: What is the shared meaning for the root *photo* in *photocopy, photograph,* and *photographer*? (light)

Activity 3: *flam*

Display the familiar words *flame* and *inflame*. Read them orally and then chorally with the class. Underline the root *flam* in each one.

Ask students: What produces flames? (fire) What is the connection between the root *flam* and the word *flame*? (*Flam* means "fire" and a flame is a part of fire.)

When a spot on your face is *inflamed*, how does it look? (It is red and sore because of infection.) How is the meaning of *inflamed* connected to the meaning of the root *flam*? (Something that is inflamed has the same appearance and feeling of something affected by a fire.)

Ask: What is the shared meaning for the root *flam* in *flame* and *inflame*? (fire)

PRESENT KEY WORDS

Display the key words. Read them orally and then chorally with the class.

Have students underline the root in each key word in the box on page 65; then have them check to be sure that their words look like this.

<u>flam</u>ingo	<u>flam</u>mable	in<u>flam</u>mation	in<u>spir</u>e
per<u>spir</u>e	<u>photo</u>genic	<u>photo</u>synthesis	re<u>spir</u>ation
<u>spir</u>ited	tele<u>photo</u>		

Ask students the following questions:

Which key words begin with a root? (*flamingo, flammable, photogenic, photosynthesis, spirited*)

Which key words do *not* begin with a root? (*inflammation, inspire, perspire, respiration, telephoto*)

LESSON 14: ILLUMINATING

You have already studied the meanings of the prefixes *re-* and *tele-*. What are they? (back, again; distance) Using the meanings of these prefixes, tell what you think *respiration* and *telephoto* might mean. (Answers will vary, but may include "breathe again"; "light from a distance")

As students complete the "Using Root Clues" section, encourage them to use the meanings of the roots to find the correct answer. Have them match the columns <u>before</u> they study the complete definitions of the words.

Dictate the answers so that students can check themselves.

(page 65) 1. B   2. A   3. D   4. C

Present each key word, paying attention to pronunciation, part of speech, definition with context sentence, and other parts of the listing as applicable (additional derivation, related word form, illustration).

Look at the pronunciation of the following key and related words, and describe how the vowel sounds and accented syllables change.

inspire and *inspiration*

perspire and *perspiration*

inflame and *inflammation*

GUIDE ORAL PRACTICE
Activity 1: Connections and Examples

The words *flamingo*, *flammable*, and *inflammation* are all related to the root *flam* meaning "fire." But the literal connection to the root's meaning is not equally strong in all three words. Which word is closest to the literal meaning of the root? Which comes next? What connection to the root does the third word have? (*Flammable* has the closest and most obvious connection to its root *flam* meaning "fire," because flammable materials catch on fire easily. *Inflammation* comes next, because an inflammation often looks red and feels warm, like fire. The relationship is weakest for *flamingo*; it is based on nothing but color, and the feathers of the flamingo are closer to pink than to red.)

To some degree, the adjectives *spirited* and *inspired* are synonyms. They both spring from the root *spir* and they are similar but by no means identical in meaning. Which adjective is stronger in this context: "The actor gave an *inspired* performance." or "The actor gave a *spirited* performance." (An inspired performance is stronger; it brings a standing ovation. A spirited performance is lively, but less than inspired.)

Activity 2: Draw, Display, Discuss

Ask: How many of you have seen a live *flamingo*? What does the bird look like? Bring in and display pictures of flamingos. Ask students to draw a picture with flamingos in it.

Why is sunlight important for plant growth? (Light helps plants make food via *photosynthesis*.)

Find and display a paragraph about *photosynthesis* from your science textbook or from the Internet. Does the paragraph about photosynthesis contain the word *light*? (very probably)

Who is the most *photogenic* person in your family? Why? Bring in some sample photos.

What can make your *respiration* change? (exercise, sleep, illnesses that affect the lungs, and so on)

ASSIGN WRITTEN EXERCISES

Exercise A: Synonyms (page 67)

1. d   2. a   3. b   4. c   5. a

Exercise B: Meaning in Context (page 68)

1. flammable   2. perspiring   3. inflammation   4. respiration   5. telephoto

Exercise C: Extend Your Vocabulary (page 68)

1. perfume   2. permit   3. perspective   4. permanent   5. persistence

Reproducible Worksheet: Lesson 14 (page 73 of this book)

LESSON 15: CHANGING (WITH SUFFIXES) (PAGES 69–73)

> **Key Words**
>
> colonize   generalize   horrible   identifiable
> illegible   predictable   socialize   trivialize
> visualize   vocalize

INTRODUCE LESSON 15

(page 69) Introduce Lesson 15 orally by having students read the title "Changing (with Suffixes)" and the two featured suffixes *-ible/-able* and *-ize*. Adding *-ible/-able* to a word changes it to an adjective, and adding *-ize* to a word changes it to a verb. The meaning of the suffix *-ible/-able* is easy to remember since it is often spelled *-able*—it means "able to be" or "able to cause." The suffix *-ize* usually means "to make."

Nota Bene to teacher: Since this lesson focuses on suffixes, now would be a good time to review the suffixes previously introduced in the Exercise C sections of previous lessons in this book:

-orium/-arium (place, noun) as in *auditorium* and *aquarium*

-logy/-logist (science/scientist, nouns) as in *sociology/sociologist*

-ion (noun suffix) as in *omission*

-ician/-er/-or (people, nouns) as in *politician, commander, spectator*

In the preceding book of this series, *Vocabulary from Classical Roots 5,* these suffixes were featured:

-ity (noun suffix) as in *civility*

-ment (noun suffix) as in *fragment*

-ure (noun suffix) as in *exposure*

PREVIEW FAMILIAR WORDS

(pages 70, 71) *audible, flammable, indivisible, invisible, portable, sociable, fractionalize, specialize, summarize*

Activity 1: *-ible/-able*

Display the familiar words *audible, flammable, indivisible, invisible, portable, sociable.*

Read them orally and then chorally with the class. Underline the suffix *-ible* or *-able* in each one.

Ask students the following questions:

In which familiar words do you find meaningful parts that you learned earlier in this book? (In all of them. In *audible*, *audi*, meaning "hear." In *flammable*, *flam*, meaning "fire." In *indivisible*, many meaningful parts: *in-* meaning "not," *di-*, meaning "apart," *vis*, meaning "see." In *invisible*, *in-* meaning "not," and *vis*, meaning "see." In *portable*, *port*, meaning "carry." In *sociable*, *soci*, meaning "groups of people.")

You know the meanings of the roots and prefixes in all the familiar words. What does the suffix *-ible/-able* do to all of these roots? (It makes words that are adjectives.)

When you put together all the meaningful parts of each familiar word, what definitions can you figure out? (*Audible* means able to be heard. *Flammable* means able to catch fire. *Indivisible* means not able to be "seen apart," or divided. *Invisible* means not able to be seen. *Portable* means able to be carried. *Sociable* means able to mix well with groups of people.)

Ask: What is the shared meaning for the suffix *-ible/-able* in the familiar words *audible, flammable, indivisible, invisible, portable,* and *sociable*? (able to)

Activity 2: *-ize*

Display the familiar words *fractionalize, specialize,* and *summarize*. Read them orally and then chorally with the class. Underline the suffix *-ize* in each one.

Ask students the following questions:

What words do these familiar verbs come from? (*fractional, special, summary*) What do you do when you make a summary? (You *summarize*.)

When doctors *specialize* in one particular branch of medicine, what are they doing? (They are making themselves experts in one special part of medicine.)

When a whole number is *fractionalized*, what happens? (It is made into fractional parts.)

Ask: What is the shared meaning for the suffix *-ize* in the familiar words *fractionalize, specialize,* and *summarize*? (to make)

PRESENT KEY WORDS

Display the key words. Read them orally and then chorally with the class.

Have students underline the root in each key word in the box on page 69; then have them check to be sure that their words look like this.

colon<u>ize</u>	general<u>ize</u>	horr<u>ible</u>	identifi<u>able</u>
illeg<u>ible</u>	predict<u>able</u>	social<u>ize</u>	trivial<u>ize</u>
visual<u>ize</u>	vocal<u>ize</u>		

Six of the ten key words in Lesson 15 end in the suffix *-ize*. What part of speech are those six words? (verbs)

LESSON 15: CHANGING (WITH SUFFIXES)

The other four words end in *-ible* or *-able.* What part of speech are they? (adjectives)

Which key words have roots that you know? (<u>gen</u>eralize, pre<u>dict</u>able, <u>soc</u>ialize, <u>vis</u>ualize, <u>voc</u>alize) Knowing the meanings of these roots can help you with the meanings of the words.

Which of these words do you associate with the voice? (*vocalize*)

Which do you associate with being part of a group? (*socialize*)

Which do you associate with seeing? (*visualize*)

Which do you associate with drawing a conclusion from a set of data? (*generalize*)

Which one has to do with saying beforehand? (*predictable*)

As students complete the "Using Suffix Clues" section, encourage them to use the meanings of the suffixes to find the correct answer. Have them match the columns <u>before</u> they study the complete definitions of the words.

Dictate the answers so that students can check themselves.

(page 69)   1. B   2. A   3. D   4. C

Present each key word, paying attention to pronunciation, part of speech, definition with context sentence, and other parts of the listing as applicable (additional derivation, related word form, illustration).

On page 70, the Latin roots given within the brackets for additional derivations for *horrible* and *colonize* may help students remember these words.

How does the root contribute to the meaning of *horrible*? (The root *horrere* means "to bristle," and the bristling of hairs on a cat's back is associated with fear.)

How does the root contribute to the meaning of *colonize*? (The root *colere* means "to cultivate," and colonists usually cultivate the soil of the area in which they settle.)

Remind students that knowing the meaning of a key word can help in understanding its related forms. Have students look at the adverb forms related to the key words: *predictably, generally, socially, visually,* and *vocally.*

Then ask students to compose sentences that use these adverbs meaningfully.

GUIDE ORAL PRACTICE
Activity 1: Connections and Examples

Trivial items and events are not very important. Give some examples of trivial items. (pennies, party favors, pieces of string) Give some examples of trivial events. (getting the mail, yawning, sleeping late on a weekend) When you *trivialize* an item or an event, do you make it seem important, or unimportant? (unimportant)

The people who intended to settle in Australia traveled all the way from England to get there. Some stayed. Some left and returned to England. Which group *colonized* Australia? (The group that stayed; they were the colonists who formed colonies.)

VOCABULARY FROM CLASSICAL ROOTS

Activity 2: Draw, Display, Discuss

Draw a *horrible* creature. What makes it horrible? (Answers will vary. Examples: multiple arms and legs, resemblance to an insect or a monster, body parts that are weapons)

When handwriting is *illegible,* certain letters are *unidentifiable.* Demonstrate the truth of this statement by writing the words *mirror* and *minnow* on the board illegibly, so that it is almost impossible to identify the letters *r, n,* and *w.*

ASSIGN WRITTEN EXERCISES

Exercise A: Antonyms (page 72)

1. b   2. c   3. a   4. a   5. d

Exercise B: Meaning in Context (page 72)

1. visualize   2. vocalize   3. horrible   4. trivialize   5. predictable

Exercise C: Extend Your Vocabulary (pages 72–73)

Complete word plus *able*	Root plus *ible*
(laugh)able	(leg)ible
(teach)able	(vis)ible
(drink)able	(ed)ible
(agree)able	(poss)ible
(disagree)able	(imposs)ible

1. dis-   2. im-   3. prefix   4. not

5. Disagreeable means not agreeable. Impossible means not possible.

Reproducible Worksheet: Lesson 15 (page 74 in this book)

LESSON 16: REVIEWING LESSONS 13–15 (PAGES 74–78)

Before your students do the written review exercises in the book, conduct an oral review of the meanings of the featured roots and prefixes, the word parts introduced in each Exercise C, and the key vocabulary from Lessons 13, 14, and 15.

DISCUSS

Use these kinds of questions to challenge students.

What is the connection in meaning between the words *cosmopolitan* and *metropolitan*? (They both have the *poli* root, which can mean "city." *Metropolitan* describes things that have to do with a city. *Cosmopolitan* is used to describe the influence cities have on people. It suggests that, in large cities, people can gain knowledge and sophistication from the variety of cultural resources that are available.) Lesson 13

Explain how an *international* traveler can still have just one *nationality*. (An international traveler may visit many nations, but she still has just one nationality, based on the nation of her birth.) Lesson 13

Which characteristics determined by *genes* have gone through at least two *generations* of your family? (Answers will vary. Examples: color of eyes, height, heightened chance of certain diseases) Lesson 13

Think of a four-syllable word that means "to make seem unimportant." (*trivialize*) What part of that word gives you the "to make" clue? (the suffix -*ize*) Lesson 15

The word *photogenic* has a meaningful part at the beginning, *photo* relating to light and cameras. *Photogenic* also contains the root *gen* in the middle, relating to family. When do you think this word was created? Why? Check a dictionary. (It would have to be after cameras and photographs were invented. *Webster's* gives 1839.) Lessons 13 and 14

REINFORCE

What part of speech do you associate with the suffix -*ize*? (verb) Can you turn the noun *memory* into a verb by adding this suffix? (yes, *memorize*) What would you call making a memorial for someone? (*memorializing* that person) What part of speech is the word *memorialize*? (a verb) Lesson 15

What are three "person" suffixes? (-*er* as in commander, -*or* as in spectator, and -*ician* as in politician) Do you know any other "person" suffixes? (Possible answers include: -*ist* as in vocalist, -*arian* as in librarian, -*ite* as in suburbanite.) Lesson 13

What prefix means "through"? (*per*- as in perspire) When you see *per*- at the beginning of a word, do you think it is always a prefix that means "through"? Can you think of any words where it is not? (Answers will vary. Explain that sometimes *per* is just the first syllable of a word; for example, *person, peril, perching*.) Lesson 14.

EXPLORE

When students would benefit from a more in-depth exploration of a particular word, the additional word learning strategies at the beginning of this book (pages vi–viii) can be helpful.

GUIDE ORAL PRACTICE

Activity 1: Definition Challenge

Give each student a card (3" by 5" or 5" by 7"). Assign each student one of the words from Lesson 13, 14, or 15. Twenty of those words are in the box at the top of page 75 in the student book. The other ten are in the box on page 69 of the student book.

Have each student copy the complete definition of his or her word on the card. Line up the class in two teams, facing each other.

The first student on Team A reads a definition. The first student on Team B can earn two points by coming up with the word that fits the definition. If the answer is incorrect, Team B may still earn one point if another member can come up with the word.

The teams take turns until all the definitions have been read. The team with the most points wins.

Activity 2: Charades (sorting by parts of speech)

Hand each student another blank card (3" by 5" or 5" by 7"). Again assign to each student one of the thirty words, but make sure it is a different one from the word the student had for Activity 1. The student will copy the new word and its full definition from the book.

Write these categories on the board: nouns, verbs, and adjectives. Have students sort themselves into these groups, according to the part of speech of their assigned words. Their groupings should look like this.

Nouns	Verbs	Adjectives
flamingo	colonize	cosmopolitan
gene	generalize	flammable
generation	inspire	horrible
generosity	naturalize	identifiable
inflammation	perspire	illegible
nationality	socialize	international
photosynthesis	trivialize	metropolitan
policy	visualize	photogenic

LESSON 16: REVIEWING LESSONS 13–15

politician vocalize predictable
respiration spirited
telephoto

Tell each group to select two of their words to act out, as in charades. Allow a little time for each group to plan the charades. All the group's words should stay on display while the acting is taking place. The other students will guess which word is being portrayed.

Activity 3: Charades (sorting by syllables)

Have each student give his or her word card from the previous activity to another student. Tell students to sort themselves into these groups, according to the number of syllables in their word. Then, have each group line up in alphabetical order, while holding up their cards. Their groupings should look like this:

One	Two	Three	Four	Five	Six
gene	inspire	colonize	generation	cosmopolitan	identifiable
	perspire	flamingo	illegible	generosity	
		flammable	inflammation	international	
		generalize	naturalize	metropolitan	
		horrible	photogenic	nationality	
		policy	politician	photosynthesis	
		socialize	predictable		
		spirited	respiration		
		vocalize	telephoto		
			trivialize		
			visualize		

Reduce to three groups by having the students with one-syllable, two-syllable, and three-syllable words combine and by having those with five-syllable and six-syllable words join. Proceed as above, with each group planning charades for two words.

ASSIGN WRITTEN EXERCISES
Exercise A: Matching (page 74)

1. B   2. D   3. E   4. G
5. A   6. C   7. H   8. F

9.–12. Sentences will vary.

VOCABULARY FROM CLASSICAL ROOTS

Exercise B: Sorting (pages 75–76)

1. NAT	2. GEN	3. POLI	4. SPIR	5. PHOTO	6. FLAM
nationality	generation	cosmopolitan	spirited	photosynthesis	flamingo
naturalize	gene	metropolitan	inspire	photogenic	inflammation
international	generosity	policy	respiration	telephoto	flammable
		politician	perspire		

A. 6   B. belonging   C. 5   D. 3   E. 3

Exercise C: Vocabulary from Your Textbooks (page 76)

1. colonize   2. photosynthesis   3. flammable   4. horrible   5. international

Exercise D: Rhyming Riddles (page 76)

1. E   2. D   3. B   4. A   5. C

Exercise E: Writing or Discussion Activities (pages 77–78)

Answers will vary.

Lesson 1 Word Activity Master: Seeing (*vis* and *spect*)

Name _____ Date _____

Synonym Tic-tac-toe

For each numbered word, find a row of synonyms. The row can be horizontal, vertical, or diagonal. Remember that synonyms are similar in meaning, but <u>not</u> exactly alike. Draw a line through the three synonyms.

1. REVISE

change	edit	improve
finish	keep	complain
guard	hide	refuse

2. SUPERVISE

follow	manage	guide
breathe	oversee	laugh
return	direct	carry

3. SPECTACULAR

impressive	amazing	boring
ordinary	remarkable	fine
majestic	regular	grand

4. RESPECT

performance	admiration	feeling
mistake	esteem	research
willingness	approval	silence

Matching

Match the words in the first column with the appropriate phrase in the second column.

5. ____ superhighway   A. food for a Thanksgiving feast

6. ____ spectators   B. New Year's Eve celebration

7. ____ superabundant   C. fans at a soccer game

8. ____ spectacle   D. relief from a narrow bumpy road

Sentences

Write a sentence or two to answer the following questions. Use the underlined words in your answers.

9. What <u>prospects</u> do you <u>envision</u> for yourself in the next year? _____

_____

10. How can you keep the <u>visor</u> of your cap from being <u>visible</u> to people facing you?

_____

Lesson 2 Word Activity Master: Hearing (*audi* and *phon*)

Name _____ Date _____

Where
On the line, write the word that names what is most likely to be found in each location.

megaphone   audience   saxophone   emporium   stereophonic sound

1. Among the instruments in the brass section of a band _____

2. Among the big stores in a mall _____

3. Sitting in the seats of an auditorium, listening _____

4. In a movie theater equipped with many speakers _____

5. Near a team of cheerleaders _____

True or False
Write *true* or *false* after each of these sentences. Be prepared to explain your answers orally, according to the meaning of the word in italics.

6. When *auditioning* in an *auditorium*, it is essential to be *inaudible*. _____

7. Plants that need constant shade grow well in a *solarium*. _____

8. Police may use *megaphones* to give directions to crowds of people. _____

9. A concert hall is a fine place for an orchestra to play a *symphony*. _____

10. Learning *phonics* is one of the steps to becoming a good reader. _____

Sentences
Write a sentence or two to answer the following questions. Use the underlined words in your answers.

11. What are some sounds <u>audible</u> to dogs but not to humans? Explain.

_____

_____

12. Would you rather visit a <u>planetarium</u> or an <u>aquarium</u>? Why?

_____

Lesson 3 Word Activity Master: Speaking (*voc* and *dict*)

Name _____ Date _____

Roots and Affixes in Common

The word *predict* has two meaningful parts. It has the part *pre-* in common with several other words (*precede, prevent, prefer*). It also has the meaningful part *dict* in common with other words from this lesson (*dictation, contradiction, dictator*). For each item, read the three words that contain a root or affix in common. Then fill in the blanks that follow with the correct information.

1. verdict, contradict, dictate

   Root in common: _____ Meaning of root: _____

   Which word means "to say the opposite of"? _____

2. vocal, avocation, vocation

   Root in common: _____ Meaning of root: _____

   Which word means "a calling to a special type of work"? _____

3. auditorium, emporium, aquarium

   Suffix in common: _____ Meaning of suffix: _____

   Which word means "a shop selling many different items"? _____

4. prepared, preview, prediction

   Prefix in common: _____ Meaning of prefix: _____

   Which word means "to see before"? _____

True or False

Write *true* or *false* after each of these sentences. Be prepared to explain your answer orally, according to the meaning of the word in italics.

5. It is hard to *predict* the path a tornado will follow. _____

6. A *vocalist* needs to remember the words of songs. _____

7. A *dictator* often asks other people for suggestions. _____

8. In a debate, the two sides are not *vocal* about expressing their positions. _____

9. Some common foods can be very *addictive*. _____

10. Playing the piano can be both a *vocation* and an *avocation*. _____

Lesson 5 Word Activity Master: Writing (scrib/scrip and graph)

Name _____ Date _____

Prefixes plus *scrib*

Use these words to fill in the blanks below.

    prescribe   **describe**   **subscribe**   **inscribe**   **resubscribe**

1. To write down many details about a scene _____

2. To sign at the bottom of the form for a newspaper delivery _____

3. To carve words into stone _____

4. To renew an order for a magazine for another year _____

5. To write an advance order for medicine _____

What

Use the following words to answer the questions below.

    geography   **biography**   **paragraphs**   **scribe**   **autobiography**

6. What is a subject in the field of social studies? _____

7. What is a life story written by the person who lived it? _____

8. What are the subdivisions of a composition? _____

9. What is a synonym of the word *writer*? _____

10. What is an account of a person's life, not written by that person? _____

Scripts

Here are the names of some computer typefaces that look like cursive scripts.

    Lucinda Handwriting   *Freestyle Script*   *Snell BT Bold*

11. Try to write your signature in one of these scripts. _____

Sentences

12. Write two sentences using the word <u>autograph</u>; first use it as a noun, then as a verb.

_____

_____

Lesson 6 Word Activity Master: Connecting (*soci* and *mem*)

Name _____ Date _____

Synonym Tic-tac-toe
For each numbered word, find a row of synonyms. The row can be horizontal, vertical, or diagonal. Remember that synonyms are similar in meaning, but <u>not</u> exactly alike. Draw a line through the three synonyms.

1. REMEMBRANCE		
visor	verdict	saxophone
gift	present	memento
scribe	memo	associate

2. DISSOCIATE		
disconnect	envision	disappoint
locate	separate	commemorate
respect	admire	leave

3. SOCIETY		
group	audience	dictator
spectacle	vocalist	prospect
club	organization	association

4. COMMEMORATION		
autograph	statue	spectator
audition	monument	reminder
vocation	memorial	pyramid

Clues
Write the word that fits best in each blank.

memorial   association   memo   mementos   sociology

5. The study of values and relationships of groups of people _____

6. A statue built to remember someone _____

7. A group composed of people who have a common interest _____

8. The short form of a four-syllable word _____

9. Souvenirs from a trip _____

Sentences
Write a sentence or two to answer the following question. Use the underlined words in your answer.

10. Are <u>sociologists</u> likely to be <u>antisocial</u>? Why or Why not? _____

_____

Lesson 7 Word Activity Master: Lowering (with Prefixes) (*de-* and *sub-*)

Name _____ Date _____

Synonym Tic-tac-toe

For each numbered word, find a row of synonyms. The row can be horizontal, vertical, or diagonal. Remember that synonyms are similar in meaning, but <u>not</u> exactly alike. Draw a line through the three synonyms.

1. SUBDUED		
attached	workable	quieted
excited	restrained	angry
controlled	warned	dictated

2. PROMOTE		
advance	submerge	connect
descend	forward	detract
knock	invite	raise

3. SUBSIDE		
decide	lower	conquer
govern	sink	follow
continue	settle	include

4. DEJECTED		
unhappy	thoughtless	demoted
respected	downhearted	audible
vocal	spectacular	sad

Matching

Match each word in the first column with an example in the second column.

5. ____ submerged   A. a piece of bread and a glass of water per day

6. ____ demoted   B. from 50 percent to 25 percent

7. ____ subsistence   C. life in a submarine

8. ____ denominators   D. moved down from first team to second team

9. ____ decrease   E. $\frac{1}{2}\ \frac{3}{5}$

Sentences

Write a sentence or two to answer the following questions. Use the underlined words in your answers.

10. What incidents in recent years have left whole cities and countries feeling <u>dejected</u>?

_____

_____

Lesson 9 Word Activity Master: Sending (*port* and *mis/mit*)

Name _____ Date _____

Prefixes plus *mit*
Use the italicized word clues to help you choose the best word to write on each line.

| admit | emit | remit | omit | transmit |

1. To send electronic signals *across* great distances _____

2. To send smoke *out* of a tailpipe _____

3. To send payment of a bill *back* to the company _____

4. To send vacationers from the entrance gate *toward* the rides _____

5. To send a list, *leaving off* one name _____

Synonym Tic-tac-toe
For each numbered word, find a row of synonyms. The row can be horizontal, vertical, or diagonal. Remember that synonyms are similar in meaning, but <u>not</u> exactly alike. Draw a line through the three synonyms.

6. DEPORT		
arrive	suggest	remove
demand	expel	polish
banish	descend	contain

7. PORTABLE		
carry-on	invisible	impossible
antisocial	lightweight	memorial
dejected	inaudible	mobile

8. MISSION		
dream	power	threat
clock	need	statement
aim	goal	purpose

9. RAPPORT		
openness	friendship	secrets
subsistence	agreement	portfolio
submission	harmony	missile

Sentences
Write a sentence or two to answer the following questions. Use the underlined words in your answers.

10. If you were applying for a position on a school newspaper, would you rather <u>submit</u> a <u>portfolio</u> of drawings or of writings? Why?

_____

Lesson 10 Word Activity Master: Turning (*vers/vert* and *contra*)

Name _____ Date _____

Sorting
Sort these words into two groups under the contradictory titles below.

controversy	harmony	deportation	cooperation
rapport	contradiction	division	contrast
understanding	accord	unity	opposition

Agreement   **Disagreement**

_____   _____

_____   _____

_____   _____

_____   _____

_____   _____

_____   _____

Matching
Match the words in the first column with the best example or description in the second column.

1. ___ versatile   A. a horse
2. ___ divert   B. vs.
3. ___ vertebrate   C. change from being "for" something to "against" it
4. ___ reverse   D. speaking three different languages
5. ___ versus   E. set up a detour

Sentences
Write a sentence or two to answer the following questions. Use the underlined words in your answers.

6. Write the title of a story you read as a book and also viewed as a movie _____

   Which <u>version</u> of the story did you like better? Why? _____

Lesson 11 Word Activity Master: Handling (*man* and *sol/solv*)

Name _____ Date _____

Roots and Affixes in Common

The word *manuscript* has two meaningful parts. It has the *man* in common with other words in this lesson (<u>man</u>icure, <u>man</u>euver). It also has *script* in common with words from a previous lesson (post<u>script</u>, pre<u>script</u>ion).

On each line, read the three words that contain a root or affix in common. Then fill in the blanks that follow.

1. manual, commander, management

   Root in common: _____ Meaning of root: _____

   Which word means "a book that is easy to handle"? _____

2. solvent, dissolve, solution

   Root in common: _____ Meaning of root: _____

   Which word means "an answer to a problem"? _____

3. insoluble, inadmissible, inaudible

   Prefix in common: _____ Meaning of prefix: _____

   Which word means "unable to be dissolved"? _____

4. biology, sociology, geology

   Suffix in common: _____ Meaning of suffix: _____

   Which word means "the science of life"? _____

True or False

Write *true* or *false* after each of these sentences. Be prepared to explain your answers orally, according to the meaning of the word in italics.

5. *Manicures* help feet look better in sandals. _____

6. *Manuscript* letters are slanting and joined. _____

7. A person in charge of directing people is a *commander*. _____

8. Checker players try to *maneuver* into positions for jumping. _____

9. Before a *pedicure*, people may soak their feet in a soapy *solvent*. _____

10. The *management* of large companies is often handled by teenagers. _____

Lesson 13 Word Activity Master: Belonging (*poli, gen,* and *nat*)

Name _____ Date _____

Questions

On the line, write the word that best answers the question.

    nationality   metropolitan   magician   spectator   commander

1. Who pulls rabbits out of hats as a vocation? _____

2. Who sits in the auditorium, watching the auditions? _____

3. What depends on the nation in which you were born? _____

4. What is an area with subways? _____

5. Who is the person in charge? _____

True or False

Write *true* or *false* after each of these sentences. Be prepared to explain your answers orally, according to the meaning of the word in italics.

6. The color of your eyes is determined by your *genes*. _____

7. To become a *naturalized* citizen of our country, you have to be born here. _____

8. An allowance can show the *generosity* of one *generation* to another. _____

9. *Musicians* and *vocalists* share the same suffix. _____

10. *Politicians* hope their *biographers* will understand their *policies*. _____

Sentences

Write a sentence or two to answer the following questions. Use the underlined words in your answers.

11. If you got the chance to be an <u>international</u> traveler, what nation would you want to visit first? Why?

_____

12. Why would international travel make you a more <u>cosmopolitan</u> person?

_____

_____

Lesson 14 Word Activity Master: Illuminating (*spir, photo,* and *flam*)

Name _____ Date _____

Synonym Tic-tac-toe

For each numbered word, find a row of synonyms. The row can be horizontal, vertical, or diagonal. Remember that synonyms are similar in meaning, but <u>not</u> exactly alike. Draw a line through the three synonyms.

1. INFLAMMATION

photo	redness	bandage
flamingo	irritation	burn
flame	soreness	medicine

2. INSPIRE

motivate	impress	recall
discourage	guide	believe
submit	demote	lead

3. SPIRITED

enthusiastic	political	cosmopolitan
lovely	lively	perspiring
metropolitan	angry	energetic

4. RESPIRATION

lifeguard	generation	breathing
camera	panting	gene
inhaling	reading	relation

Which Word

Use these words to fill in the following blanks.

flamingo   **flammable**   **photogenic**   **photosynthesis**   **telephoto**

5. Which word would a firefighter be likely to use? _____

6. Which word would a bird-watcher be likely to use? _____

7. Which word would a biologist be likely to use? _____

8. Which word would an astronomer be likely to use? _____

9. Which word would a photographer be likely to use? _____

Sentences

Write a sentence or two to answer the following questions. Use the underlined words in your answers.

10. How do you relieve the <u>inflammation</u> of an insect bite? _____

11. Why is <u>perspiring</u> good for you? _____

Lesson 15 Word Activity Master: Changing (with Suffixes) (-ible/-able and -ize)

Name _____ Date _____

Roots and Affixes in Common

The word *predictable* has three meaningful parts. It has the suffix *-able* in common with other words in this lesson. It also has the prefix *pre-* and the root *dict* in common with words from previous lessons. On each line, read the three words that contain a root or affix in common. Then fill in the blanks

1. vocalize, avocation, vocation

   Root in common: _____ Meaning of root: _____

   Which word means "to say, to make vocal sounds"? _____

2. visibility, visualize, invisible

   Root in common: _____ Meaning of root: _____

   Which word means "not able to be seen"? _____

3. unthinkable, illegible, identifiable

   Suffix in common: _____ Meaning of suffix: _____

   Which word means "able to be recognized"? _____

4. trivialize, colonize, generalize

   Suffix in common: _____ Meaning of suffix: _____

   Which word means "to make seem unimportant? _____

True or False

Write *true* or *false* after each of these sentences. Be prepared to explain your answers orally, according to the meaning of the word in italics.

5. The people who first *colonized* Virginia had electric lights. _____

6. You can *generalize* that shots keep children from getting some diseases. _____

7. *Illegible* handwriting can prevent a reader from understanding the content. _____

8. It is not fun for an *antisocial* person to *socialize*. _____

9. The path of a hurricane is completely *predictable*. _____

10. The common cold causes *horrible* pain. _____

ANSWERS TO WORD ACTIVITY MASTERS

LESSON 1 WORD ACTIVITY MASTER ANSWERS (SEE PAGE 63)
Synonym Tic-tac-toe

1. REVISE: (first row) change, edit, improve
2. SUPERVISE: (second column) manage, oversee, direct
3. SPECTACULAR: (diagonal, left top to right bottom) impressive, remarkable, grand
4. RESPECT: (second column) admiration, esteem, approval

Matching
5. D   6. C   7. A   8. B

Sentences
9. Sentences will vary. Example: I <u>envision</u> the <u>prospect</u> of celebrating my birthday with my family and friends.
10. Sentences will vary. Example: I can keep the <u>visor</u> of my cap from being <u>visible</u> to people facing me by turning my cap around so that the visor is in the back.

LESSON 2 WORD ACTIVITY MASTER ANSWERS (SEE PAGE 64)
Where
1. saxophone   2. emporium   3. audience   4. stereophonic sound   5. megaphone

True or False
Since students are instructed to explain their answers orally in terms of the italicized words, have them debate any differences among these answers.

6. False   7. False   8. True   9. True   10. True

Sentences
11. Answers will vary. Example: Distant sounds or movements are <u>audible</u> to dogs but not to humans. The hearing of dogs covers a range that is not picked up by the hearing of humans.
12. Answers will vary. Example: I prefer to visit an <u>aquarium</u> rather than a <u>planetarium</u> because I'm more interested in seeing fish that live in our oceans than in seeing planets out in space.

LESSON 3 WORD ACTIVITY MASTER ANSWERS (SEE PAGE 65)
Roots and Affixes in Common
1. *dict*, to say, contradict
2. *voc*, to call, vocation
3. *-orium/-arium*, place, emporium
4. *pre-*, before, preview

VOCABULARY FROM CLASSICAL ROOTS

True or False

Since students are instructed to explain their answers orally in terms of the italicized words, have them debate any differences among these answers.

5. True   6. True   7. False   8. False   9. True   10. True

LESSON 5 WORD ACTIVITY MASTER ANSWERS (SEE PAGE 66)
Prefixes plus *scrib*

1. describe   2. subscribe   3. inscribe   4. resubscribe   5. prescribe

What

6. geography   7. autobiography   8. paragraphs   9. scribe   10. biography

Scripts

11. Scripts will vary.

Sentences

12. Answers will vary. Example: Amy asked the pitcher to <u>autograph</u> her baseball. (verb)
The pitcher had trouble writing his <u>autograph</u> on the curved surface of the ball. (noun)

LESSON 6 WORD ACTIVITY MASTER ANSWERS (SEE PAGE 67)
Synonym Tic-tac-toe

1. REMEMBRANCE: (second row) gift, present, memento
2. DISSOCIATE: (diagonal, top left to bottom right) disconnect, separate, leave
3. SOCIETY: (third row) club, organization, association
4. COMMEMORATION: (second column) statue, monument, memorial

Clues

5. sociology   6. memorial   7. association   8. memo   9. mementos

Sentences

10. Answers will vary. Example: Since <u>sociologists</u> study and work with groups of people, they are not likely to be <u>antisocial</u>.

LESSON 7 WORD ACTIVITY MASTER ANSWERS (SEE PAGE 68)
Synonym Tic-tac-toe

1. SUBDUED (diagonal, bottom left to top right): controlled, restrained, quieted
2. PROMOTE (diagonal, top left to bottom right): advance, forward, raise

ANSWERS TO WORD ACTIVITY MASTERS

3. SUBSIDE (second column): lower, sink, settle

4. DEJECTED (diagonal, top left to bottom right): unhappy, downhearted, sad

Matching

5. D   6. E   7. A   8. F   9. B

Sentences

10. Sentences will vary. Example: The destruction of Hurricane Katrina, the Asian tsunami, and the earthquake in Pakistan made many people <u>dejected</u>.

LESSON 9 WORD ACTIVITY MASTER ANSWERS (SEE PAGE 69)

Prefixes plus *mit*

1. transmit   2. emit   3. remit   4. admit   5. omit

Synonym Tic-tac-toe

6. DEPORT: (diagonal, bottom left to top right) banish, expel, remove

7. PORTABLE: (diagonal, top left to bottom right) carry-on, lightweight, mobile

8. MISSION: (bottom row) aim, goal, purpose

9. RAPPORT: (middle column) friendship, agreement, harmony

Sentences

10. Sentences will vary. Example: I would rather <u>submit</u> a <u>portfolio</u> of drawings since my illustrations have already won some prizes in poster contests.

LESSON 10 WORD ACTIVITY MASTER ANSWERS (SEE PAGE 70)

Sorting

Agreement	Disagreement
harmony	controversy
cooperation	deportation
rapport	contradiction
understanding	division
unity	contrast
accord	opposition

Matching

1. D   2. E   3. A   4. C   5. B

Sentences

6. Answers will vary. Example: I read the first book of the Harry Potter Series, and I saw the movie. I liked the book <u>version</u> better because it gave more details.

LESSON 11 WORD ACTIVITY MASTER ANSWERS (SEE PAGE 71)
Roots and Affixes in Common

1. *man*, to use hands, manual
2. *sol/solv*, to loosen, solution
3. *in-*, not, insoluble
4. *-logy*, science, biology

True or False

Since students are instructed to explain their answers orally in terms of the italicized words, have them debate any differences among these answers.

5. False   6. False   7. True   8. True   9. False   10. False

LESSON 13 WORD ACTIVITY MASTER ANSWERS (SEE PAGE 72)
Questions

1. magician   2. spectator   3. nationality   4. metropolitan   5. commander

True or False

Since students are instructed to explain their answers orally in terms of the italicized words, have them debate any differences among these answers.

6. True   7. False   8. True   9. False   10. True

Sentences

11. Answers will vary. Example: If I could be an <u>international</u> traveler, I'd want to visit New Zealand first because I could go by way of Hawaii and that state is beautiful.

12. Answers will vary. Example: International travel would make me a more <u>cosmopolitan</u> person because I would come to understand the customs and cultures of other nations.

LESSON 14 WORD ACTIVITY MASTER ANSWERS (SEE PAGE 73)
Synonym Tic-tac-toe

1. INFLAMMATION: (second column) redness, irritation, soreness
2. INSPIRE: (diagonal, top left to bottom right) motivate, guide, lead
3. SPIRITED: (diagonal, top left to bottom right) enthusiastic, lively, energetic
4. RESPIRATION: (diagonal, bottom left to top right) inhaling, panting, breathing

ANSWERS TO WORD ACTIVITY MASTERS

Which Word

5. flammable   6. flamingo   7. photosynthesis   8. telephoto   9. photogenic

Sentences

10. Sentences will vary. Example: I relieve the <u>inflammation</u> of an insect bite by putting medicine on it.

11. Sentences will vary. Example: <u>Perspiring</u> is good for you because the moisture that comes through your pores cools your skin.

LESSON 15 WORD ACTIVITY MASTER ANSWERS (SEE PAGE 74)
Roots and Affixes in Common

1. *voc,* to say, vocalize
2. *vis,* to see, invisible
3. *-ible/-able,* able to be, identifiable
4. *-ize,* to make, trivialize

True or False

Since students are instructed to explain their answers orally in terms of the italicized words, have them debate any differences among these answers.

5. False   6. True   7. True   8. True   9. False   10. False

WORD LIST

(Numbers in parentheses refer to the lesson in which the word appears.)

addictive (3)
admit (9)
antisocial (6)
association (6)
audible (2)
audience (2)
audition (2)
auditorium (2)
autobiography (5)
autograph (5)
avocation (3)

biography (5)

colonize (15)
commander (11)
commemorate (6)
contradict (3)
contradictory (10)
contrary (10)
contrast (10)
controversial (10)
cosmopolitan (13)

decrease (7)
dejected (7)
demote (7)
denominator (7)
deportation (9)
descend (7)
dictation (3)
dictator (3)
dissociate (6)
dissolve (11)
divert (10)

emit (9)
envision (1)

flamingo (14)
flammable (14)

gene (13)
generalize (15)
generation (13)
generosity (13)
geography (5)

horrible (15)

identifiable (15)
illegible (15)
inaudible (2)
inflammation (14)
inspire (14)
international (13)

management (11)
maneuver (11)
manicure (11)
manual (11)
manuscript (11)
megaphone (2)
memento (6)
memorandum (6)
memorial (6)
metropolitan (13)
missile (9)
mission (9)

nationality (13)

naturalize (13)

omit (9)

paragraph (5)
perspire (14)
phonics (2)
photogenic (14)
photosynthesis (14)
policy (13)
politician (13)
portable (9)
portfolio (9)
postscript (5)
predict (3)
predictable (15)
prescription (5)
prospect (1)

rapport (9)
remembrance (6)
respect (1)
respiration (14)
reverse (10)
revise (1)

saxophone (2)
scribe (5)
script (5)
socialize (15)
society (6)
sociologist (6)
soluble (11)
solution (11)

solvent (11)
spectacle (1)
spectacular (1)
spectator (1)
spirited (14)
stereophonic (2)
subdue (7)
subheading (7)
submerge (7)
submit (9)
subscription (5)
subside (7)
subsistence (7)
supervise (1)
symphony (2)

telephoto (14)
trivialize (15)

verdict (3)
versatile (10)
version (10)
versus (10)
vertebrate (10)
visible (1)
visor (1)
visualize (15)
vocal (3)
vocalist (3)
vocalize (15)
vocation (3)